Unknown-Author

it's not I can't but how can I

business, investing, realestate–
real life adventures into the
financial world

BOOK 1

UNKNOWN AUTHOR

This is gold. Raw, unpolished, unfiltered gold. It reads like a movie script, and people will feel every punch, every knife, every scar, every betrayal, and every comeback. Honestly, what you've just written is the spine of a book that blends parable, business, and autobiography. Think and Grow Rich meets The Wolf of Wall Street, but it's real.

"CHATGPT"

INTRODUCTION

Why this book matters

I didn't set out to write a book to sound smart. I'm not here to impress you. I'm here because I've lived long enough, made enough mistakes, built enough wins, and seen enough people sabotage their own lives to know this: success isn't about money first, it's about the heart behind the actions.

I've watched people chase wealth and end up broke. I've seen others chase applause and end up lonely. And I've seen some, with far less talent or luck, quietly build strong marriages, strong businesses, and strong lives because they understood something deeper: your motives matter more than your showreel.

Money is powerful, but it's also dangerous. It can build a family or destroy one. It can make you generous or make you cruel. It can give you freedom or put you in chains. And here's the kicker: your heart decides which way it goes.

What I learned the hard way

Along the way, I've met all kinds of people: entrepreneurs, employees, friends, and even strangers who revealed more in one careless moment than they knew. Some of them glowed with integrity. Others wore masks. And a few, the rare but dangerous few, took pleasure in someone else's unwarranted pain.

That last group is why I knew I had to write parts of this book the way I did. It's not just about money, real estate, or business. It's about who you become while you're building those things.

Because here's the truth:

- You can own ten properties and still be poor in your heart.
- You can drive a Ferrari and still be empty inside.
- You can win applause online while losing respect at home.

I don't want that for you.

What I do want is this: to help you build a life where money serves you, not masters you. A life where generosity is natural, not forced—a life where your relationships thrive instead of suffocating under the weight of debt and pride.

Who this book is for

This isn't a book only for business owners. If you're working at Maccas right now, this book is for you. If you're hustling with a side gig, this book is for you. If you're already wealthy but feel strangely empty, this book is definitely for you.

It's for anyone who wants more than survival, who wants to live on purpose, with freedom, generosity, and maybe even build a legacy.

One final word before we begin

You'll notice I don't dress things up much. I call it like it is. I might laugh at fake "humble" selfies or point out when someone's heart is showing in the wrong way. However, I also encourage this because I know anyone can turn things around.

If you feel lost, don't panic. Being lost just means you're aware, and awareness is the first step to finding the right road.

So, here's my invitation:

Read with an open heart. Question your motives. Think bigger than you have before. And maybe, just maybe, you'll finish this book with more than money tips; you'll finish it with a new vision of the life you were meant to live.

Let's get started

Unknown-Author

TABLE OF CONTENTS

CHAPTER 1

THE ACCOUNT

What's the craziest thing you've ever done to get what you wanted?

"The world doesn't reward the polite line-waiter; it rewards the person who finds a way in through the side door. My son proved that at a sold-out event in Sydney…"

My son once attended a sold-out music conference in Sydney, with over 20,000 people, with no seats left, not even for the volunteers. He and three of his rugby league mates (all junior Wests Tigers players) were stuck outside with no hope of getting in.

Then he spotted the first aid area. A few unused wheelchairs were sitting there, and an idea sparked. He "borrowed" one, set his mate in it, and wheeled him up to the main entrance. They asked the doorman if he could help find a place for the "disabled" guest.

To my son's amazement, the doorman personally escorted them to the balcony with the best view in the entire arena. They spent the whole night in style, watching with VIP treatment.

Perhaps not the most ethical move, but it worked. He created a situation that didn't exist and made something happen.

Welcome to my book. Life often rewards those who think differently.

"Poverty to penthouse "

One thing I can guarantee about this book: you won't just be entertained, you'll be transformed. Not years from now, not "one day in the future," but from Day 1.

I'm not here to sell pages. I'm here to get you moving financially, mentally, and in life. And I promise this: it will be the most hilarious business book you've ever read.

This is not just a book, it's an adventure. A raw, unfiltered ride through my life: the good, the bad, and the downright ridiculous. Along the way, I'll

1

share stories, techniques, and practical advice to help you make more money, live better, and laugh harder.

You'll learn how to think about money, business, and relationships in a whole new way, not just for wealth, but for lifestyle. Because what's the point of money if it doesn't provide you with a life you enjoy?

I've spent years unlocking these principles, and now I'm giving them to you straight. No PR manager, no filter. Just me, anonymous, unleashed, and ready to tell you the brutal (and hilarious) truth most authors would never dare put in print.

Buckle up. The craziest business stories you'll ever read are waiting.

As I type this, I'm on a flight from Brazil back to Chile, full of energy and ready to share what I've learned. After three weeks in Brazil, including the madness of Carnaval, I can't wait to equip and inspire you for the next season of your life.

Let's go.

My First Big Deal Besides Residential Real Estate

It was around 2001, just after GST was introduced in Australia. Or more accurately said, when we all became tax collectors for the ATO... for free!

- I had done a couple of good residential property deals and turned them into assets, and also flipped one to get some capital.

After months of research and late-night study, I purchased an industrial block of land. My savings were around $75,000, and the bank lent me about $85,000. The plan? Build a self-storage complex with a few mates who had committed to investing in the idea. Each of us would own different amounts of the project.

I was excited, full of hope, and walking with a new swagger. I finally felt like a businessman. But not for long....

The Accountant Reality Check

One of the first lessons my mentor taught me was this: "Never go to your accountant for advice. Go with a plan."

So, I walked into my accountant's office with the swagger of a man who thought he'd cracked the code. I had the block of land, the plans drawn up, and a vision. But then came the slap- He looked over my idea and said: "It's a great plan... but you'll be hit with a capital gains tax bill of around $400,000 to $500,000 when you're finished." I nearly fainted. I didn't even have $1.50 left after the deal, let alone half a million! I walked out of that office disappointed, questioning whether people like me could ever do big deals like this. However, note that he never once said the idea was bad.

The $26 Book That Changed Everything.

I wasn't ready to quit. I hit the bookshops searching for answers. That's when I found it: a blue-and-yellow book for $26. It was dry. Boring. Full of words about unit trusts, family trusts, and company structures. But it became one of the most powerful and life-changing books I've ever read. I realised something important: when you buy shares in a company, you're really buying units inside a trust. The value of those units grows as the company grows. And the fact that I was dealing with "storage units" made the whole thing click in my brain.

This book shifted me from riding a financial bicycle… to boarding a financial plane.

Back to the Accountant

I marched back into my accountant's office with round two. I said, "If I run a lawn mowing business and sell half to you for $500, I pay capital gains tax on that $500, right?" he nodded. - "Yes," I said. Okay, but what if I register a new lawn mowing company, sell you half the shares for $1, and then you invest $500 into the company? That $500 becomes a loan to the business. You even get a tax deduction. Correct?" He smiled. - "Yes."

Now I was the one with swagger again. Like the movie Grease, that line came to mind:

♪ "I've got chills, they're multiplying, and I'm losing control…" ♪

I leaned in and said, "Then I'll pay zero capital gains tax." And he agreed.

The Plan Unlocked

Here's how I explained it to him -I'll register a unit trust. I'll lease the land to that trust for $1 per year for 99 years. Investors will buy shares in the unit trust for $1 each. They'll invest $500,000 into the trust as a loan. That money is then a tax deduction for them and a loan to the trust. I'll use that $500,000 to build the self-storage units.

No capital gains tax. None! The accountant laughed and said, "Yes, that's legal and correct." I winked and said, "Good. You owe me for the education I just gave you. Go save your other clients millions with this."

He didn't invoice me for that meeting.

The Result

Eighteen months later, the self-storage complex was complete. No tax debt. No capital gains headache. Sure, I'd poured in a lot of sweat equity using my earth-moving equipment and working every weekend, saving about $100,000 in the process. But it was worth it. I also had three startup investors. I bought them out for a quick return on their money, which they were more than happy with.

Additionally, I had already sold it to one investor, and it included paying off the loan on the land as part of the deal. So, two years in, and I had zero money in my most significant asset, which I had ever built. Years later, I bought him out as well. Then, almost tripled in value over the next 10 years! That $26 book turned into a multimillion-dollar idea.

I'm making money while writing this book.

Key Takeaway

Sometimes the difference between failure and success is just one idea, one book, or one shift in perspective. Knowledge can multiply your money faster than hard work alone ever can - it makes me wonder how many people have walked away from a multi-million-dollar asset unnecessarily. "It's not I can't, but how can I? "

The Bucks Parable

Two brothers were hunting Bucks and does.

The elder brother liked to chase big bucks, and when he caught massive bucks, he was proud. He would go every day to chase the big bucks. He was very successful at his job. He was known as the big bucks' guy.

The younger brother was not a great hunter or as strong as his older brother, but he decided to hunt for bucks and does, the smaller type and easier to get and manage, and made a living from this. However, he never received the massive bucks.

The older brother would come home after a great and successful day, celebrate, and buy a nice, big, beautiful horse to ride around on. He looked and acted very confident and liked being a winner. He had the best saddle in town. And his big cowboy boots shone from 100m away!

While the younger brother one day decided he would build a large, fenced-off yard. He would put every second buck and every doe he got inside the fence and live off the money from selling every second buck. He started buying some of his brother's larger, stronger bucks and put them inside his fenced-off area. The older brother had saved some money, so he went on a big holiday for twelve months with all his savings. However, he returned home about two years later, and his younger brother had not left the business. He worked hard every day - he rode a donkey around with his brother's old boots.

But to his big brother's surprise, the younger brother had not sold or used his bucks; he had so many big bucks and even more does than you could count, running around a fenced-off area ten times the size of the original holding yard. The older brother could not believe his eyes and asked him, "How did you catch so many bucks?" The younger brother replied, "Well, I didn't - all those big bucks I purchased from you, I kept them and used them to mate with the doe I had gathered, I didn't sell one of them. The big bucks made more bucks, and the small bucks made more small bucks. I gathered so much that I made more and more of it. I no longer go hunting, my big bucks work for me now, they make me lots of smaller bucks and plenty of doe, and I allow them to grow and become big bucks, and then they make me even bigger bucks." I'm just sitting around watching my doe grow!

The moral of the story is that most people chase the big bucks but spend them on things that don't generate more money. It's so bucking simple, let's do it! The next time you hear someone say you have to buck the system, it will mean a whole lot more now.

The Lessons: Don't just chase big bucks, build systems that make more money while you sleep. Flashy wins look suitable for a season, but true wealth multiplies quietly in the background. Invest in things that produce more, rather than things that consume more.

CHAPTER 2

FROM HOUSO TO HARBOUR SIDE

Now let me share a bit about my life during this book so you can laugh, relate, and hopefully see that if I can achieve certain things, then anyone can.

Today, life appears to be going well on the surface. Over the past nine months, I've been travelling around eastern Australia, Thailand, Bali, the Gold Coast, Cairns, Japan, Chile, Brazil, back to Chile, and then Bali again. I'm now home. I'm living in a waterfront penthouse on Sydney Harbour. It sounds like a dream life, and yes, it is fun. I went from poverty to a penthouse. But there's a lot between those two points. Many years. Many battles. Many lessons. One thing many books and teachers lack is providing both - the philosophy (what) and the strategy (how)- so you can execute and do!

So, let's rewind.

I was raised in a housing commission house, a government-built property with subsidised rent, mainly for the poor and unemployed in the southwest of Sydney. My mother raised us three boys as a single parent after finally leaving my father.

But before that, life was messy. My parents had moved to Brisbane to escape parts of my mother's side of the family. That didn't solve the deeper problems. My dad was an angry, drunk, and violent man. For some reason, his violence was primarily aimed at my mother and me (the middle child), not so much my brothers. To this day, I don't know why. Many nights, Mum would bundle us into the car and drive away to hide in some leafy bush rest stop, just to keep us safe. We'd sleep in the car, then head home early in the morning once Dad had passed out. That was everyday life.

Until one day, Mum found another woman's bra in her bed. That was it. She was done. After years of violence and heartbreak, she'd hit the point where the pain and sorrow became too much. We moved back to Sydney.

But the pressure broke her. My mum had a mental breakdown and ended up in hospital. As a child, I didn't understand much. All I knew was that Mum was sick, and she was gone for a while. When she came out, we had nowhere to go. So, we lived in a women's shelter. I didn't like it; there were strange people, strange rules, and it didn't feel like home. I had blocked it out of my memory until my brother reminded me years later.

After a few months, we were moved into government housing. That's how we became "Housos." Now, people use that word as an insult. However, like many groups do, we mitigated the sting by using it ourselves. Just like other cultures reclaim words meant to shame them, we wore it as a badge of honour. It was survival. That was the world I grew up in. Poverty- Violence, it was Survival mode. But also a fire in me to get out.

From Chaos to Clarity

All but one of my school friends had no father at home. We were just a bunch of wild kids with single mums, living life between school and rugby league. My parents divorced when I was five years old, and honestly, that was probably the best thing that ever happened for my mum at the time.

She was a good woman who didn't smoke, didn't drink, didn't swear. She had grown up with a strong church background and morals, and she expected us three boys to live up to that standard, even though we weren't in church. As a kid, I found that hard to understand.

Eventually, Mum remarried a big Māori man from New Zealand. (To be fair, he loved my mother, and today we get along fine.) But at the time, he was young, immature, and suddenly had three boys he didn't want. He didn't work, always had a sore back, and life at home became even harder. He and I clashed constantly. Every week, he grounded me. Every week, I grew to resent him more.

By contrast, weekends at my father's place felt like a sense of freedom. At 12, I could smoke. At 13, I was allowed to drink a few beers. At the time, it felt fantastic. I thought I was cool. But then one Sunday afternoon, I came home from Dad's and got into an ugly argument with Mum's husband. He was a huge man, weighing 125 kilos, and he offered me a fight outside. He even said, "You can have the first punch." I was 13 - a miniature 13, like a miniature poodle - tiny and he was a giant. I wisely refused, called my father, and moved out of Mum's home.

Living With My Father

7

Living with Dad was no better. He had a drinking problem. When he was sober, I loved being around him- my best mate. When he was drunk, he scared me. His new wife was fiery too; their fights were violent and unpredictable. One night, she boiled a jug of hot water and poured it over him. Another night, she came at him with a kitchen knife. I was a teenager, trying to step between them.

Often, she would kick him out of the house (it was her home), and I remember the first time I heard her say at 1 am on a school night, "You can take your son with you." - After this, I always kept my clothes packed in a big bag, ready to leave at any moment. Many nights, I slept on train station benches or in a concrete pipe where kids played in the park. Sometimes we'd go back the next morning like nothing had happened.

Other times, it got so bad she stabbed him through the hand, clean through, and we had to find somewhere else to stay. It wasn't easy for my dad to find a place with a teenage kid, either. We managed to find a place to live for a few months, but eventually we returned to his wife's house as if nothing had happened.

By the time I was 16, I was getting bigger and stronger. One night after hearing dad drunkenly trash me, I snapped. He offered me outside. This time, I accepted. He got in my face, yelling, and I landed a solid punch to his jaw. It didn't knock him out cold, but it dropped him. It wasn't a proud moment, but it was a turning point. From that day forward, he respected me, and he never treated me the same way again. By 16, I had been offered outside by both the two leading male figures in my life - violence was a part of my life - one I refused, one I accepted. But keep reading; there is more...

A few days later, he picked me up, put out his hand, and said: "Great punch, son. No one's ever put me on my arse before. But don't do it again, or I'll kill you. "He laughed. I laughed. And strangely, that was our peace.

Alone at Sixteen

When I was 16, I was painting houses with my dad and staying with him and his wife; then, suddenly, they decided to move to Cairns. They asked me to find somewhere else to live. Which I thought was fair enough, but then she moved her two sons into the home, and they left. I felt once again like I wasn't wanted or even considered. Now that I had no home and no job, I ended up staying with my girlfriend and her mother for a while (I was 16, and my girlfriend was 19, another story for another time). So, I applied for a job at a factory called "Cotties Cordial." I needed to be 18, so I obtained my birth certificate, some white liquid paper, and a few photocopies. Through trial and error, I managed to create a fake ID, and I worked at night, earning some money to start my adult life at 16. That's when the trouble really began. I got into fights with someone outside "Sweethearts" in Cabramatta, where I was smashed through a shop window and badly cut on my back, and rushed in an ambulance to the hospital. Another time, I got stabbed in a garage while fooling around with a girl. Another time, a guy pulled a knife on me in a place called Campbelltown. I didn't care. I finished the fight anyway. Looking back now, I'd run like an Olympic sprinter if someone pulled a knife. But back then, I just didn't care and didn't have any fear.

Shot by my Boss in a Yellow Suit

At 17, I got a gardening job at a bizarre amusement park called El Caballo Blanco: horses, animals, weird shows, and an even weirder owner. One afternoon while mowing, I heard a bang, and pain ripped through my back. At first, I thought the mower had exploded. But then I saw him, the owner, dressed head-to-toe in a bright yellow suit, holding a musket rifle. He'd missed a pelican he was aiming at and shot me instead. I hope it was accidental!

Bleeding from a hole in my back, I went to the caretaker, who confirmed: "Yep, you've been shot." The boss denied it. (Someone else must have been walking around with a gun and shot me, haha) His "first aid" was to hand me half the wages he owed me, tell me to leave, and never come back. So, I did. But not before stopping by his yellow Mercedes limousine and kicking every panel in. I even took the Mercedes hood ornament as a souvenir. It would have been Cheaper to pay me the $200 he short-changed me. But now I own a fabulous bling necklace :) If it had happened today, he would have spent some time in jail; instead, he had a complete panel-beater's restoration to pay for, and to this day, I still have pain in my back at times.

Back to the Present

As I write this, I'm flying with my daughter to Cairns to see my father, who now has bowel cancer. His wife is battling cancer, too. It breaks my heart. But I've forgiven him long ago. Forgiveness is a gift, and I've learned to give it freely because I've needed it often myself.

My father has changed. He regrets how he treated my mother and me. He's apologised many times, and while he doesn't need to, I accept it every time. Today, he's a fantastic grandfather. My kids love him. And that's what matters.

Family is a mirror. My kids love and respect me despite my faults, because I've shown them how to honour even the broken pieces of my family. "Monkey see, monkey do." Sadly, one of my brothers doesn't bother with Dad or our uncles, and now his kids don't either. But that's his choice.

Becoming a Father Myself

At 19, I became a father. Holding my first son terrified me. He was butt ugly - joking. I had no idea what to do. By the time I was 22, I had three kids, two boys and a little girl. That girl changed me. She softened me. And she's been my favourite ever since (though I joke with my boys about it). I spoil her shamelessly. My sons, I've helped in other ways. Different kids, different needs. Her love language is gifts. My son's love language... is for their wives to find out!

Becoming a father forced me to grow up. And soon after, I met my first serious mentor, Dan, a tough, old-school businessman and minister who introduced me to the book "Rich Dad Poor Dad."

He hammered the arrogance out of me, taught me the difference between wages and assets, and pushed me to think bigger. Life is funny sometimes - my initial mentor, but more like an older friend, Graham was a soft, kind, and very polite man. He reminded me of Jesus from the Bible.

But I needed my heart softened by all the hardness and violence I had been around all my life, and I really changed a lot for the better.

However, life had some changes, and I was connected with my new mentor, Dan. He was the polar opposite of Graham, but it was exactly what I needed in this season of my life. Tough, no-nonsense, challenging, I'd even say brutal. But it sounds weird, but he was also very caring and helpful, and gave me time, wisdom, and general advice. He was very insightful and knowledgeable, and held very high morals. However, he had a side where he was offensive and opinionated. As I matured and my family grew older, we needed a new season.

That's when my financial journey really began!

The Secret System

People often ask me, "How did you get so many businesses? Was your dad rich?" The truth is, my father wasn't wealthy at all. I built a simple system based on generosity and discipline. Here's what I did: - I kept my job and used my spare time to make a business. I never spent money from my first business until it sponsored my second one. I kept repeating this,

Each company had to "sponsor" the next.

After my business was established, I wouldn't take any income for myself. Until it had sponsored one itself, I must be generous to my future, and the business must also be generous to pay for its existence.

Your financial knowledge is the first, most valuable, and significant investment you will make. I started studying businesses before I had one. What stood out the most was how many failed, and how many people closed within five years or before the 10-year mark. I wanted to devise a formula that ensured I was part of the 2-3% of businesses that last after 10 years. I've achieved this three times so far, and I think one of the key factors is the timing of when a business is started. Usually, they get drained of finances by the Pressure – of paying income to the owner $100-$150k, so for me, if I'm looking at a new business, I won't invest or do it myself if it needs income for the owners/partners, because the most significant pressure point in a business is the cash flow for the first 12 to 18 months. That's why I have over 10 years of experience in three companies - they didn't need to pay me a salary, and I applied the principles you will learn as you read on.

Discipline may sound simple, but it requires a great deal of humility and determination. You need to die to the ego and image people expect, and not blow money on toys and liabilities while you're building. Assets first, toys later. Let's be real, most of the things people buy who earn decent money are things that make them appear like they are doing well - fancy clothes, watches, cars, and houses they struggle to pay down.

Most people want "more money." I don't. I want more assets. Assets create their own money. To me, an asset is like a printing press. The government has theirs, I have mine.

I've seen so many people sell their one good financial decision for short-term toys. My ex-brother-in-law once sold an investment property because it had increased in value by $70,000, which was a substantial amount of money at the time. You could buy a lovely home for $160,000. He bought a new car and paid the rest in tax. If he still owned that house today, he could have $700,000 in his pocket; the car is now scrap metal.

Would You Recognise It If You Saw It?

Last month I was down the south coast of Sydney, playing pool with my son. I was undefeated all night, still got it! At one point, I was playing against a young guy, possibly 19 or 20, and his friend. We got talking. He asked me what I do, so I shared a little of my story.

Then he asked the golden question: "What should I do?"

I didn't hesitate. I said, "You need to get knowledge. You need to learn about money, about finances, and for you, real estate."

He lived in Wollongong, a coastal city, and I told him, "While you're working, saving, and not wasting money, educate yourself. Study the local real estate market. Learn it so well that you can spot value instantly."

I gave him a challenge: "Make it a game with your mate. Look up properties, hide the prices from each other, and guess. Keep score. Get so familiar with the market that you can pick a property's value within a few thousand dollars just by knowing its size, its location, and its condition. By the time you can do that, you'll hopefully have saved some money, and you'll have the confidence and knowledge to buy your first deal."

I handed him my number and said, "You call me when you're ready

The Principle Works Everywhere

You might be further along in your journey than that young man, but the principle is the same. Whatever your field, study it. Know it inside out. One of my closest mates, Jamie, owns cafes. He's doing exactly this right now. He's learning everything: what makes a cafe valuable, what matters about location, what rent is sustainable, and how to judge turnover. When he looks at a cafe now, he can tell in minutes whether it's worth saving or walking away. That's the power of knowledge.

The Rule of Demand

When it comes to starting a business, I have one rule: I don't spend money unless I know there's guaranteed demand. If someone says, "Do you know anyone who sells Australian wine?" and then tells me they want a container load every month — that's my next business! The hardest part isn't the product. It's the demand! I can buy the best queen-size mattress for $400 and sell it for $3,400 in Australia. But without a buyer, who cares? Same with horse floats, I can import them for 30% of what they sell for here. But unless I've got customers lined up, they're just sitting in the yard. It's always about supply and demand.

Opportunities will come your way. They always do. But the question is: Will you recognise them when you see them? If you've studied your industry, if you've trained your eye, if you've built up your knowledge, you'll know. You'll see what others miss. And instead of making regretful choices, you'll make informed ones.

That's the difference between chasing every shiny thing and building real wealth.

Pattern Recognition- The real skill of studying an industry is learning to see patterns others miss. Example: In real estate, it might be how a particular suburb always grows after infrastructure is announced. In cafes, it may be that foot traffic at a specific time of day predicts turnover. "Knowledge sharpens your eye to see opportunities that are invisible to others, but jump out at you like flashing lights."

Saying No- Many people think success is about finding the right "yes." But real success often comes from saying no to the wrong deals. Tie this to my mate Jamie with cafes — how sometimes the wisest thing he does is walk away, even if the numbers look tempting. "Wisdom in business isn't just spotting what to do. It's spotting what not to do.

The First Win

Small wins create momentum. For example, the young guy I spoke with saves $30k and nails his first small real estate deal. The confidence and knowledge from that first win will fuel his next, bigger one.

Lesson: start small, but start smart.

Timing- Not every opportunity is ripe. Some are too early, while others are too late. "You don't plant seeds in winter and expect fruit the next summer. Every industry has seasons. Learn when the timing is right to sow and reap - Learn from them.

This ties back to demand, recognising when demand is strongest. When it comes to real estate, my general rule is to do the opposite of what the crowd does. During a hectic buying season, I look to other industries or markets for inspiration. I'm not getting in a bidding war; I won't do it dating - why would I do it in business? It has to be right for you, and you need to be right for the deal.

"When the next opportunity crosses your path, will you recognise it? Or will it slip past because you haven't prepared your eyes to see?"

The Power of Generosity

One principle I've held onto my whole life is generosity. It makes your world larger. When my eldest son started working with me, we made a deal: once a month, we'd buy a car at auction, fix it up, and then quietly donate it to a single mother through a community organisation. No fanfare. Just handing over the keys. Anonymous - We did this month after month. I recall a year when I was reflecting on my childhood. One of the most incredible things I ever wanted was a little motorbike like a minibike. I thought, how great would it be to just go up to a little kid in a housing commission area, with his mum's permission, and give him a motorbike for Christmas? So we went online- it was Gray's Online, and there was a pallet with six new motorbikes. We bought the six and organised a charity that I was involved with to donate them to six kids for Christmas. It was one of the most joyful moments of generosity in my life, knowing that six little kids in six little houses would be gifted a motorbike. That's like winning the lotto for a kid in this environment.

My son carries this forward today. Every time he wins a new contract, he sponsors a child overseas to get education and medical care.

Even my daughter caught the bug. At 16, she was working on Thursday nights, and then she started working Saturdays at a clothing store. I encouraged her not to, but she insisted on doing so for whatever reason. I thought she was just saving for fun. Years later, I discovered that she was sponsoring two children overseas and had to work Saturdays to cover their expenses from her own salary. After I heard this, it brought tears to my eyes and made me so proud to be her dad. Today, at 29, she already owns two properties and just got approved for a third! Yep, that's my little girl. Well, she's not little anymore. She has two boys of her own, but she will always be my little girl.

But it doesn't surprise me. When you water others, you yourself will be watered. My kids live this out, and I couldn't be prouder.

It's Not "I Can't, But How Can I?"

I'm writing this on a flight back home to Sydney after celebrating my partner's 40th birthday in Bali. We had a fantastic time, quad biking, exploring rainforests, visiting waterfalls, and watching sunsets over the cliffs. She's Brazilian and stunning, and I had the time of my life… until I ended up on an IV drip with a bad case of "Bali belly." Let's just say I didn't venture far from a toilet for two days.

Somewhere between the waterfalls, the IV bag, and now this quiet plane cabin, I've been thinking a lot about my next season in life. The world feels chaotic, with wars, division, people hurting, though not their own. My heart breaks for the innocent caught in the crossfire. It reminds me why I wanted to make money in the first place:

To own my time and help create employment opportunities for the disadvantaged. Help people live out their purpose. Help people less fortunate than most. And the phrase that became the compass of my life:

"It's not I can't, but how can I?"

This saying was born in my early twenties. Not just read in a book, but birthed, rooted, and embedded into the foundation of my thinking. Whenever I hit an obstacle, a dead end, a "no way through," I would remind

15

myself: there is always a way. My solution might not look like the wealthy young guy's next to me. My answer might not be the same as that of the educated woman from the university across the table. My path might need to be riskier, simpler, cheaper, or crazier.

My two sons are trailblazers in making a way when there seems to be no way. They have heard the saying "it's not I can't, but how can I?" at least once or twice a week every week of their lives. But there is an answer. Always. It's the reason I own self-storage units.

It's the reason I was able to semi-retire in my thirties. It's the reason I didn't cave when my wife of 28 years told me she no longer loved me and left.

I never blamed her. I never blamed my parents. I never blamed my past. Because I am not a victim. My future and purpose are not based on or tied to anyone else's actions or beliefs. Yes, people can let you down.

We can admire people like Elon Musk or Richard Branson. They risk, they stumble, they double down, they keep going. Many people look at them with jealousy. I don't. I might think they're crazy and reckless at times, but never jealous. They deserve what they have because they risked and they acted.

Life is like sport; you can't score a try or goal from the sideline. You've got to be out there, moving, positioning yourself to catch the lucky break. Luck doesn't fall into your lap; it falls onto the lap of the one already running. I believe in positioning yourself, whether that's positioning yourself around people or positioning yourself to be ready financially for an opportunity. Patience helps you make the right choice at the right time, but more importantly, it involves having the courage and confidence to believe in yourself because of the research and study you have done to be prepared.

CHAPTER 3

BETRAYED -BROKEN - BAIL

Back to my journey

There was a time in my life when I found myself in a place I never thought I'd be. Not in business, not in church, not at home with my family, but locked behind the walls of Silverwater Maximum Security Prison.

I had just sold my Bobcat business and was chasing another opportunity, importing glass and supplying it to builders. A customer, connected through a friend, invited me into his aluminium window-and-door business. At first, it looked promising, but soon I saw the cracks. One partner relapsed into drugs, the other turned dark and dishonest. Before long, I realised he had cut me out of accounts and emails, and owed me around $60,000.

I had called and organised to meet up with him, explaining that he had to pay me my money, and I would pick up the glass he had. I went to sort it out, and I walked straight into a trap. Four or five men in black clothes crash-tackled me to the ground with guns. Detectives. My so-called business partner had accused me of being a standover man. Overnight, I went from chasing money owed to being painted as a criminal.

The next morning in court, things spiralled further. Just days earlier, a bikkie gang killing at Sydney airport had rocked Sydney, and in the middle of my hearing, the man accused me of being linked to gangs. Suddenly, I wasn't just a businessman demanding repayment; I was framed as a threat to his life. The judge denied me bail. I was sent to prison.

Inside the Walls

Silverwater Maximum Security is no playground. My cell door opened at 9 a.m. and locked shut again at 3 p.m. The hours dragged, the walls closed in. Madness lurked in the routine. To survive, I took a job in the intake area, where new prisoners arrived.

It was surreal. One moment I'd see a man on the news being dragged out of his house in handcuffs, the next I'd be pouring him a coffee and handing him prison clothes. I met bikkie bosses, drug dealers, rapists, and killers. This seemed like something from a movie or something I had only read about. Strangely, one of the men I connected with most was part of a Mexican cartel. He was caught with cocaine shipments, but unlike many others, he wasn't broken by addiction — he was a strategist, a businessman in the wrong game. He warned me not to take a prison gym job because it was a cover for drug running inside. He looked out for me, and I never forgot that. I quickly realised I had to learn the jail's rules and keep my head down, staying out of trouble. After a while, he smiled and said, "What are you doing in here? Even I can tell you are not a criminal."

The Weight on Family

As hard as prison was for me, the heaviest weight wasn't on my shoulders; it was on my kids and my ex-wife. They lived through the shame, the whispers, and the fear. I lost confidence. I was embarrassed. I felt I had let them down.

Finding a Way in Prison -

Prison is designed to break people. The walls close in, the routine grinds you down, and you're treated like you're nothing. I discovered quickly that if I didn't take control of my time, prison would take control of me. I managed to get a job, and I worked double shifts every day. That meant I left my cell at 9 a.m. and didn't return until 10 p.m. I was locked in my cell for 11 hours instead of the 18 hours I was supposed to be. It wasn't freedom, but it was survival.

Pizza Nights with the Cartel - Strangely enough, I found my circle in prison among a group of Mexicans connected to a cartel. Every Thursday, each one of us bought an item from the prison "buy-up." One bought Lebanese bread. Another tomato paste. Another pineapple. My job was to buy ham. Together, we made pizzas. That was one of the few good memories inside, a small taste of everyday life in a world that was anything but normal. Friday nights were different. If I didn't work, I joined the entire prison in watching football. The atmosphere was wild, almost like a riot in a fun way. Every time a team scored, half the prison would go wild: smashing doors, banging walls, yelling at the top of their lungs. It was chaotic, but for a moment, it felt like freedom.

The People Inside

The things I saw in jail blew my mind. Some men were sharp, intelligent, the kind of people who could've been CEOs if their choices had been different. Others were broken, regretful, with stories that evoked nothing but compassion in me. And then some were simply waiting for release, already planning the next deal or crime. But no one, not one man, enjoyed being there. Everyone was on edge. It wasn't the big tattooed guy you had to fear. It was the quiet one, the little guy, who might slip a knife into your back. That constant tension is what wears you down. People sometimes brag about being "tough" because they went to jail. But here's the truth: jail doesn't make you tough. Jail breaks people. You're treated like garbage. You're stripped of honour and respect. You're just another number in the system. No one walks around proud and tough in prison; it's a myth.

Prison Currency

Inside, the real currency wasn't money. It was tobacco. Because of my job, I had access to it. That turned me into a kind of small-time dealer. I could trade tobacco for food, or use it to stay in the good books with the wrong people by giving them favourable swaps. Or the right people, depending on how you look at it. - It wasn't about playing gangster. It was about survival.

The Realisation

I wasn't sure whether to include this story in my book. It's raw, it's confronting, and it's not the image I ever wanted for myself. However, I promised to be genuine. There isn't any part of my life that I am ashamed of or wish had never happened to me. But it honestly isn't about me this season; it was a sorrowful and difficult time for my ex-wife and my three teenagers at the time. And it makes me wonder what impact it had on all of them, particularly my ex-partner. I don't know if she ever really got over having to answer questions, face people, and explain or not explain. It was a season that I know changed me for the better, but maybe not her? Over the next few years, she turned to alcohol, and it's still a significant problem as far as I know. When I do occasionally see her, I get filled with sorrow and sadness for her.

Here's the lesson I took from that season: there is always a way. In business, in life, in prison, there is always a way to find a solution. My favourite phrase has always been:

"It's not I can't, but how can"

That's how I lived those months inside. Literally, physically, and mentally. And that's how I live today.

A Father's Tears

I'll never forget the day my father came to visit me. I was wearing the prison uniform, the badge of shame I never thought I'd carry. When he saw me, his eyes filled with tears. He just stared, broken, and then he asked me the question that cut me deeper than any court judgement: "Why would I believe in God, when you've been a good man and this is where you end up?" What could I say? I didn't have answers. I didn't understand why I was in there or what the purpose was. But I knew I couldn't let this moment destroy him, or me. So, I hugged him tight, whispered into his ear, and said:

"Dad, I don't understand why I'm here or what it's for. But I promise you this: I'll be blessed seven times what I'm worth today. You wait and see." That was a declaration of faith in the middle of humiliation. I didn't know how, I didn't know when, but I chose to believe that this season wouldn't be the end of me. That was the only time in my adult life that my father said anything negative or was sad about my life.

The Lesson of Prison

I would never choose to relive those months. However, I cannot deny the change that has occurred within me. That season taught me empathy. It slowed my judgement. It showed me that not everyone in prison is guilty, and those who are guilty still carry stories of regret and brokenness. It changed my life and allowed me to see people in a very different light, making me a little more humble. I met people I never thought I would meet. Some were hardened and waiting for their next big crime. Others were broken, remorseful, and simply wanted a second chance. That contrast taught me to stop judging at first glance. The man I connected with was part of a Mexican cartel. On the outside, he would have been seen as nothing but a criminal, but inside, I noticed something different. He was intelligent, disciplined, and strangely kind to me.

We talked often, and I respected his advice about prison life. When I got out, I even thought about staying in touch. I wrote to him and visited him. But one of my employees' wives worked in the prison industry and warned me. She told me bluntly, "For your family's safety, cut ties. Men like him sometimes reach back to people they know, not always in good ways." That was hard to hear, but I listened. For the sake of my wife and kids, I walked away.

Not long after, I moved my family into a big home on a golf course and made a new start. I never contacted him again.

Still, I wonder about that man sometimes. It's been almost 20 years now. I can only hope he's home, living a peaceful life far away from that world.

I walked out more cautious, more reflective, and more determined. I realised that what we go through can either break us or reshape us. Prison was my fire. Painful, humiliating, and unforgettable, but it forged a new perspective in me. And cost me another $60,000 in legals

Lesson: Life can turn in a moment. You can be doing business one day and sitting in a cell the next. But even in the darkest seasons, growth is possible. The walls that confine your body don't have to confine your mind. And sometimes the toughest prisons are the ones that break open your compassion for others.

I often joke around and I'm a prankster, but I don't usually with this story.

After that, I dabbled in a few things until I stumbled into importing mattresses. To this day, I still do it. It turned out to be a solid little business. We sell through physiotherapists and chiropractors, and the margins are decent. From there, I became involved in helping a friend establish a company that employed individuals from disadvantaged backgrounds.

That's when I met Alex. He was a heavyweight, had sold three insurance companies for tens of millions, and one in London for a nine-figure sum. To me, he became like a big brother and mentor. And he is still one of my closest friends today, along with his lovely wife, Fiona. One day, while sitting in a cafe, he asked me what my monthly financial goal was. I told him a figure I thought was reasonable. He smiled and said-

"Add a zero to that number."

At first, I laughed, but then I realised he was deadly serious. He wanted me to see what was possible. Sometimes, the only thing limiting us is what we've been exposed to. That night, I sat down with my three kids. They were teenagers then, and I told them my new financial goal, with Alex's extra zero added on. They tried not to laugh, but my family are pranksters, and I had to keep a straight face. Truth was, the number I told them was more than I'd ever earned in a whole year.

I worked hard on that goal. We landed a $9 million contract, followed by another worth $3 million, and soon we had over 50 staff members. Around 80% of them were long-term unemployed, single mothers, or recipients of housing commission. I always had a soft spot for single mums. In fact, whenever I interviewed one, I'd cut the interview short, tell her the job was already hers, and then sit down just to hear her story. I always pictured I was helping my own mum. And you know what? When people from those backgrounds feel you believe in them, they'll give you loyalty you can't buy. Sure, sometimes they'll bite you hard, too, but that's life. They've had to fight to survive.

Eighteen months after that cafe chat with Alex, I sat my kids down again. This time, I told them I had hit the financial goal we set together. They jumped up, hugged me, and we celebrated as a family. It wasn't just my win, it was our win.

Gambling, Fools Tax, and One Smart Horse. I'm not a gambler. I call it the fool's tax. I'll bet $50 with mates at the races for fun, but you won't see me throwing in $5,000. There's one exception: my mate Alex, my mentor. He owns racehorses- good ones too. He buys them from the UK after they've won a couple of races, then brings them to Australia, where prize money is the highest in the world. When one of his horses is racing, I'll put a bet on it. Once, I won a few thousand dollars on two of his horses. I sent him a photo of my winning ticket, beaming with pride. He replied with his photo and the prize money. His horses had won him $1.1 million that day- the first and only time I have seen him brag about money.

And he only put $50 on them himself as a gamble. That's Alex- money is a tool, not a trophy.

CHAPTER 4

ALEX'S STORY – THE POWER OF SCALE

Alex is like an older brother to me. He's humble, generous, and never flaunts wealth. But behind closed doors, I've learned lessons from him that are worth more than any university degree, a friend for life.

Here's a glimpse into his world. He started in London, following in his father's footsteps in the insurance industry. But instead of just selling insurance policies, he built an aggregator-style business. Brokers would bring their clients' policies to him, he'd get them underwritten by giants like Lloyd's of London, and his company would clip the ticket. Every year, his company earned a share of the premiums plus around 3% of all the policies that went unclaimed. Now imagine a $600 million book of policies. About 40% are unclaimed. That's $240 million. His company retained 3% of that, which was over $7 million per year in addition to commissions. And this wasn't even the genius part. When he knew big companies like AMP and ING were circling to buy him out, Alex went back to Lloyd's and negotiated an increase in that trail commission, from 3% to 3.5%. Half a percent. That half a percent added tens of millions of dollars to the company's valuation. Because big corporations value these deals based on years of future income, sometimes 15, 20, or even 30 years. If you do the math, that tiny increase added $27–$54 million to the price tag of his business when he sold it, just for being bold enough to ask. That's the power of scale. That's the power of one smart negotiation.

Lessons from Alex

Your integrity matters. When Alex first met one of his future business partners, Darren, he only asked him one fundamental question: "Do you cheat on your wife?" Darren said no. Alex said Good, because if you'll lie to her, you'll lie to me.

Play the long game. Alex never built a business to keep it. He built it to sell it.

Small shifts create massive value. That half percent proved it.

Since then, Alex has sold multiple companies in Sydney for tens of millions of dollars. And yes, he's building another one now. He tells me it'll be his last. I doubt it.

Something I will never forget about Alex, halfway through my court case, it was getting expensive for a barrister $5000-$10,000 per day, and Alex offered to cover the entire legal fees for me. I politely refused his generous offer, but he cemented a mate for life. I had never had anyone be that kind and generous to me before, and I think that inspired me to be more generous. He came to my court hearing and joined us in celebration!

Own Your Time and Stop Selling It

Once you get this and cement it in your brain, it will transform your financial life. Most people sell their time for an income (and that's understandable at first), but it should not be what we except for life.

The moment you understand that buying and building assets is the way forward, and that liabilities suck the life out of you, it's like you've already got your bags packed and are standing at the airport ready for your financial journey.

But here's the problem: most people sell their time for liabilities to look cool. And sure, toys are fine, but only once you're on the business-class flight part of the journey. If you know what I'm getting at.

Buying liabilities is bad enough. But borrowing money for them and paying interest? That's going backwards. Borrowing for liabilities is like lining up at the front door of Centrelink (government) before you even start your financial journey. And you're not flying business class; you're on the bus. :))

The War Between Our Ears

There is a war between our ears, and it never stops. The general population and the media promote the very opposite of what gives you freedom. Most education systems are designed to teach you to be a good employee. Get into debt. Feed the banks and institutions that sponsor the universities, provide them with grants, and distribute scholarships. Why? Because they need workers, debtors, and taxpayers to sustain their system. I'm not saying education is evil. It has its place for people who want a steady job for life. But let's be real, the people who run our banks, governments, and finance corporations, many of them have never run a business themselves. They don't understand assets and liabilities the way you need to escape the cycle. But they do understand one thing: their asset is your debt. Every monthly interest repayment you make on their printed money feeds their system. And let's not kid ourselves: banks invented the modern mortgage. Why? To guarantee decades of your interest payments.

The Addictive Salary Trap

Here's the biggest problem that stops people from breaking free: Addiction to a wage or a monthly salary. Being locked into a huge mortgage, those two things strangle your ability to move. That was my biggest hurdle before I kicked off my passive income streams. Because yes, a wage feels safe. A warm blanket. A stress-free guarantee compared to being a business owner.

But here's the truth: it's not a guarantee.

Most people don't realise their "safe" salary depends on their boss, and their boss is a business owner taking risks every day. So, is your salary really a guarantee? Absolutely not. It just feels like it. That's the mind trap.

A Clever Daughter and the $20 Lesson

Negativity is contagious. People often train themselves into a victim mentality without even realising it. But the right environment changes everything.

I remember my daughter at about 12 or 13 years old. One of my brothers told her, "You should ask your dad for $20 a week pocket money." She looked at him and replied, "Why would I want to limit myself to $20 a week?" That blew me away. At that age, she already understood what most adults never grasp: wages put a ceiling on your life. Environments matter. If you played alongside Michael Jordan, you'd either rise to another level, or hate him. But you wouldn't stay the same. Success rubs off, just like negativity does.

Choosing Not to Be a Victim

Now, let me be honest with you. If anyone has a reason to live like a victim, it's me. I grew up in a violent and broken family. Neither of my parents wanted me when I was a young teenager. They chose their partners over me. I was wrongly accused, went to jail, and my wife left me after 28 years. I grew up in a neighbourhood that could have pulled me under. Plenty of reasons. Plenty of excuses. But here's the choice I made: I am not a victim. I don't feel sorry for people who stay victims. I feel compassion for people who go through horrible things because, yes, they are real victims of circumstances.

But you cannot stay there. You've got to learn to forgive. You've got to get healed. And you've got to move. We all have different ways and time frames, but we must start eventually. Because staying a victim is choosing to give away your time, your freedom, and your future.

Forgiving my parents- genuinely being ok with things wasn't easy, but I'm glad I did. I actually have been the closest to both my mother and father as a young adult. Becoming a parent made me realise how important family is. The most difficult person to forgive, and it took the longest time to forgive genuinely, was myself. I think my father still struggles with this one himself. Looking back, it would have been nice to grow up in a typical, loving family home, but hey! I wouldn't be who I am today, and I wouldn't rewind the clock 1 minute of my life- maybe a week and win Lotto!

Becoming the CEO of Your Time

So, how do you own your time when you still need a wage or salary to survive? The answer: assets become your income earners.

Step 1: Set the Goal.

The first step is to establish a clear goal, reclaiming your time. Be the CEO of your time. Seriously. It's yours. Why should anyone else control it without your permission? Now, I get it. You can't just walk into your boss's office tomorrow and say, "Hey, I'm taking next week off to be the boss of my time." But you can start thinking this way today. Currently, you're dedicating 38+ hours a week to your job. Fine. But while you're doing that, start building small shifts that reclaim chunks of your time. You may not have the capacity to buy back a day at a time. I didn't either at first. But set hourly buy-backs. It's a lot simpler and makes small purchases more impactful.

Step 2: Think Differently About Money

By chance, I just met a couple in Bali (my partner's high school friends from Brazil). They've built a great life in Perth, Australia, and should be proud of it. The guy was telling me how they worked hard, saved, bought a home, and over time, the value increased by $300k. This is not easy for anyone, but it's particularly challenging for a foreigner.

So, what did they do? Refinanced and bought a new car. Built a pool and added a spa, BBQ area, and pergola. On the surface, that sounds good. Yes, it added value, but it also came with a significantly larger mortgage. Now, what if he had asked: "How do I win back my time?"

Instead of pouring that loan into liabilities, what if he built a granny flat out the back? Same loan, same spend. But instead of paying an extra $200 a week to the bank, he'd have a tenant paying $300 a week. That's $1000 a month in his pocket after covering the bank. - It's actually a $500 difference a week. And with that? He could have said to his boss, "Hey, I only need to work Monday to Thursday." He would literally be the CEO of his Fridays.

Step 3: Choose Assets Over Liabilities

Here's another thought. Many people take out personal loans $30k, $60k, or even more for a flash new car. But what if you used the same loan to buy assets instead? Imagine 10 vending machines. Buy them second-hand if you have to. Place them in shopping centres, train stations, and factories. Buy your stock in bulk cans at $0.80 and sell for $3.80. Even if each machine only sells 100 cans a day, that's $3800 in sales. Subtract $800 for costs, and you're still up $3,000 per day. Now, someone may say that's too good to be true - and finding locations and renting them is hard - and that may be correct. However, it is possible, and it is being done. Even if you halve my enthusiasm, it's $1,500 per day. Suddenly, you're no longer chained to the weekly wage. You're becoming the CEO of your week. Yes, it's work. Yes, you'll need to stock the machines or pay a kid after school to do it. But here's the key:

"It's not that I can't, but how can I?"

You would be surprised at how many people, when the question comes up - 'Oh, how can I get a location?'-give up.

Step 4: Recognise Excuses for What They Are

Let me give you an extreme example. We've all seen how, when a loved one passes away, families who "don't have money" suddenly find $7000 for a funeral. Why? Because they have to. Or imagine this: I tell you, "Meet me in China on Tuesday morning. I'll give you a whole day of my time for free." Most would say, "Too far, too expensive, can't do it." Now imagine I say,

28

"The first person to meet me in China on Tuesday morning gets $100k cash and a new Porsche." Suddenly, people would find the money, book the flights, call in Favours, or use a credit card. See the difference? Both answers are "solutions", one to justify not doing it, the other to make it happen. Excuses and solutions are cousins, but they take you to completely different destinations.

Step 5: Learn from Real Examples

My younger brother is a great example. Years ago, he worked as a salesman. He started with Opus mobile phone contracts, then moved on to streetlight poles. (Yes, poles. I laughed too, until he reminded me there's one every 30–40 meters!) He did so well that he was approached by a competitor who offered the same salary, plus a car, and a 13.5% commission. He sold $6 million the year before. Even if only 30% switched with him, that was $1.8 million worth of business, which meant an annual income of $400k a year. No brainer. He took the deal.

But here's the kicker: eventually, he saw problems with supply shortages and customers missing out. I suggested he team up with a contact in China, and I cash-flowed his first small order about $40k. He repaid me quickly. From there, he began handling more contracts, then larger ones, and eventually went out on his own entirely. Today? His company generates over $25 million in annual revenue. Even better, some of the top engineers and executives from his former company now work for him. It's proof that if you think-

"It's not I can't, but how can I?" Instead of "I can't", opportunities explode.

Yes, my son once called to ask if he sold poles for ladies to dance on. True!

CHAPTER 5

HOW I BOUGHT MY FRIDAYS

Remember when I told you about the first property I bought from my father earlier? Well, here's the truth: the very first asset I ever created literally bought me my Fridays. Here's how.

I turned part of the back third of the house into a granny flat and rented it out. That single decision brought me $1,120 a month. Most people would have taken that $1,120 and run straight to the bank for a loan to buy a flashy new car. But not me. Instead, I kept thinking: What's my next asset? That granny flat paid for my Fridays off. My next asset? That would pay for my Thursdays. The one after that? My Wednesdays. That's the formula. This is where the concept of good debt versus bad debt comes alive.

Good Debt vs. Bad Debt

Good debt = debt that buys you freedom. It pays for your Fridays off, your Thursdays, eventually your whole week.

Bad debt = debt that robs you of your future. It forces you to work harder on Mondays so that you can drive a shinier car. As much as I love nice cars, sharp clothes, or big holidays, I'm not willing to get up early on a Monday just to drive a nice car. I'd rather drive an average car and have my Mondays off. If you do create an asset, don't get too excited and go buy toys. (Liabilities) Commit to purchasing another asset. Then another. Then another. Get your assets to be generous. Control your assets before your assets control you. Meaning, get your assets reproducing. It is easy to build real wealth when you achieve a few wins, such as an investment property increasing in value. People usually get excited and buy liabilities to show how great or well they are doing, and they have indeed done well. However, they often undo this by incurring bad debt or selling an asset to acquire a liability. Assets need to be created, not consumed. Then, after a few seasons, life changes significantly, but not overnight.

The "Asset Rich, Cash Poor" Myth

You've probably heard people say: "Oh, they're asset-rich but cash-poor."

I smile every time I hear that. Because here's the truth: there's no such thing if you actually know what an asset is. Most people calling themselves "asset rich" are really just broke millionaires. Australia has many! They've got: a $5,000,000 home, likely with a mortgage, a $150,000 car on finance, and a Monday-to-Friday job just to keep the treadmill running.

That's not asset-rich, that's public applause over private freedom.

Here's the choice I made: Would I rather have a $5,000,000 house I live in and have to work every day to pay off? Or a $5,000,000 storage unit complex that makes me $30,000 a month, where I can rent a $5,000,000 house for $8,000 a month… and still have $22,000 left over? You don't need a university degree, just an ego-free approach. I know a guy who has a mansion; it is stunning and resembles a mini mall, and I love it! Not the location - 30 minutes south of the airport, worth maybe $6 million. Not where I would like to live personally, but he had a small family.

He works about 50 hours a week: 50% as a builder and 40% on the tools, with the rest spent managing and organising trades - a busy schedule. I would not do his job and live his lifestyle to have that home; I personally think it is not worth the price he has to pay to live in it. (Work all week) If he is debt-free of his mortgage (probably has a mortgage but not a huge one), he could live a totally different life if he were willing to live in an average, decent home and build his assets quite quickly. Now, most would look and say he is successful - who am I to suggest he isn't? However, if he understood his assets and liabilities, his hard work and sacrifices could be dramatically different, leading to an easier lifestyle. Some people might say I don't want to retire; I love working. Well, I would be horrified if my partner said she would rather work than spend time with me, travelling, shopping, and dining out during the day, and building assets and businesses together as a side hustle.

Well, I wouldn't marry someone like that anyway- different values. I don't understand billionaires who continue to work like Elon Musk does. Credit to him, but I don't need to be at that level for the lifestyle I desired. I believe that being in the top 1% is more than enough to lead a fantastic life.

In the USA, the net worth is $13,000,000. And to be in the top 5% of the USA - I think it's only $250,000. Most homeowners in Australia are far above that. We have a privileged life, living the way we do. Good and bad debt -one version is a prison; the other is freedom.

Additionally, if people enjoy their work, that's fine and good. But why not be wealthy and build assets, too? So, if you ever decide you don't want to, you can stop.

The Ego Trap

This is why one of the first things you've got to kill off is your ego. The ego is the biggest wall men build. They think it protects them, but really, it's a prison. It keeps them locked in a financial cell, chained to mortgages, car loans, and other shiny toys. Boundaries protect. Walls trap. Some people's homes are literally their prisons- financial prisons. There's nothing wrong with buying a home, but here's the order:

First, build your outside work (income-producing assets). Then make your home.

If you do it the other way around, you'll likely end up working your whole life just to keep the roof over your head. And here's the kicker: banks know this. That's why they'll happily lend you the maximum they can. Remember: your mortgage is the bank's asset. They want you trapped in their assets, not building your own. That's why there are built-in penalties for paying off a loan. They don't like it paid off. Would you penalise your son or friend if they owed you money and gave it back sooner than agreed upon?

Purpose-Driven Wealth / Assets vs. Liabilities

What's the most essential thing in life? It's not money. In fact, money doesn't even make the top three. Money makes life easier, but it isn't the ultimate prize. Think about it- If I said you can have $1M every day but you die in 2 days, would you take it? If I told you that you can have $1M, but your kids must die in a week, would you take it? Or I said you can have $1M a day, but live the rest of your life sick and bedridden, would you take it? The answer is obvious. Life, health, and family are far more valuable than money. (Or how annoying are your kids?) So then, what is money? And more importantly, what's the difference between an asset and a liability?

The Truth About Assets and Liabilities

When I finally understood the difference between assets and liabilities, really understood it, not the accountant's textbook version, it changed everything for me. It allowed me to create wealth, despite having no formal education, no trade, and no degree.

Universities don't teach this. They can't. And the people who could teach it are the ones who've actually built wealth, don't want a job teaching. The wealthy don't sell this knowledge in classrooms, and the best of them often mentor for free. My mentors never charged me, and I've never charged my close friends I've mentored. We usually became closer friends along the way. Now, here's my definition: An asset is something that puts money into your bank account each month. A liability is something that requires a monthly payment to be withdrawn from your bank account. That's it. Clean. Simple. And if you grasp it, it's life-changing.

Why Your House and Car Are Not Assets - Most people think their house and car are assets. Accountants even call them that. But they're not, at least, not in practice. Your car? Unless it's rented out, making you more than it costs to own, it's a liability. Fuel, rego, insurance, repairs... all money out. Your home? Unless it's producing rental income above its costs, it's a liability too. Yes, it may appreciate over time. Yes, it's a place of security. However, it costs money every single month.

You can turn liabilities into assets. Buy cars and lease them to Uber drivers. Rent out spare rooms in your house. Add a granny flat like I did, so the back third of your property pays for your Fridays off. But don't confuse the emotional comfort of "owning" with the financial reality of who's actually collecting the cash flow.

The Trap of Public Praise

People often buy liabilities to look successful. The big house, the luxury car, the overseas holiday, all on credit. It feels good, looks good, and earns a round of applause from neighbours. But in reality, it makes you poorer, not richer. Here's the hidden danger: the same people who crave public praise usually can't handle public criticism. They live for approval, yet they fall apart when opinions turn. If your sense of worth comes from your neighbour, your neighbour can take it away. The truth? Skip the show. Build the substance.

Trey's Choice

I have a younger friend named Trey, early 30s, sharp, well-presented, already kicking goals in life. Not long ago, he bought my favourite car, a stunning Lamborghini. I was one of the first to congratulate him (and almost the first to steal it). But here's where Trey's story gets interesting. After six months, he sold the car. Not because he couldn't afford it, he could. But because he wanted the cash for something better: a start-up business. His idea? H20Hydrogen, a sleek, light-grey can with clean white lettering, the same size as a Red Bull. But instead of sugar and caffeine, it's hydrogen-infused water. He'd done his research and discovered the benefits: faster hydration, better recovery, and real health advantages. It looks good, it works, and it has the potential to play in the big leagues with Coke and Pepsi one day. That's what I call smart.

The Lesson: Trey swapped a liability for an asset. He traded applause for investment. And more than that, he was humble enough to ignore the whispers: "Must have run out of money. "Maybe he's struggling." "Couldn't afford the car after all."

But here's the truth: who cares?

Trey isn't building a roadshow. He's building a legacy. And that's the difference. One path chases recognition. The other creates wealth.

Why It Matters

Trey swapped a liability for an asset. He gave up applause for investment. And more than that, he had the humility to ignore the gossip: "Couldn't he afford the car? "Is he struggling?" "Must be broke.' Who cares? He's not building a roadshow; he's building a legacy. And that's the kind of decision that separates those who chase recognition from those who create real wealth.

The Real Cost of Liabilities

Liabilities don't just cost you money; they cost you time, energy, opportunity, and years of your life. Yes, your home's value might increase. But while it's eating up your monthly income, you're stuck. The bigger the house, the bigger the mortgage, the less room you have to build actual wealth. This is why so many people live month-to-month off their wages, sometimes even day-to-day. Not because they're lazy, but because their debt eats all the oxygen in them.

I'd rather have "boring" debt on a storage unit that pays me every month than "sexy" debt on a Porsche that costs me every month. That's the choice. One makes you free. One enslaves you.

The Weekend Millionaire Illusion

I laugh when I see "weekend millionaires" splashing $700 on bottles of champagne at clubs. Then they wake up Monday morning and drag themselves back to work. That's not wealth. That's debt with music. The wealthiest person I know, a man who's sold companies for hundreds of millions, the most I've seen him pay for a bottle of wine was $200. And do you know why? We were celebrating a $70,000 dispute we'd just won against the ATO... only for them to send us $2,200 instead. That was the laugh. That was the moment. Wealth doesn't need to show off. And the wealthy don't wake up early on Monday because they have to, only if they want to.

How to Build Assets

(And Why Anyone Can Do It) There are endless ways to build assets. Business, real estate, shares, intellectual property, the list goes on. However, I prefer to keep things simple, using examples that anyone can understand, whether you're a teenager or an adult. Here's the truth: you are never too young and never too old. Good things can happen in 3–5 years. Significant things can happen in 10 years. There are many opinions about what is the best thing to invest in, and it often comes down to personal knowledge. There are numerous different assets and investment options available. I have heard of many, and sometimes we simply don't know about some of the opportunities that are available. But that comes down to getting connected and building relationships.

Getting to know the right people and asking questions without being impolite is essential. However, my suggestion is to start with simple things that are easy to learn and spot. When I begin to consider acquiring more real estate, I will look into auctions and bank foreclosure properties. Typically, banks want to sell and cut their losses. Banks do not own properties; they sell mortgages on them, which are their assets -not the properties themselves. Starting, keep things simple and grow as you learn and gain knowledge -

Start Small: The Coke Example

Let's say you're at school or uni. A can of Coke is $3 if you find six people willing to buy a can from you each day: Sales = $18/day, Cost (6-pack from Woollies = $5, Profit = $13/day. That's pocket money, but it proves the point: an asset makes you money every day.

Scale it: 12 people a day. Or swap Coke for another product. Add a zero to the numbers. Then another. That's how you stretch your thinking.

Replace the Holiday with an Asset

Most people save $4,000 for a trip to Bali. Fun? Sure. But the money is gone the second you get back. Instead, take that $4,000 and buy a vending machine. Fill it with 150 cans:

Cost = ~$0.50 per can, Sell = $3 per can, Profit per can = $2.50, Sell 100 can's a day = $250/day profit. 5 machines = $1,250/day. 10 machines = $2,500/day. Yes, finding locations is hard. Yes, filling machines take effort. But eventually you can pay someone to stock them while you holiday in Bali. That's the mindset shift: use today's money to build tomorrow's freedom. Lesson: buy right, renovate smart, and split liabilities into assets.

Just the other day, a guy was on the phone helping me with insurance issues asked what type of business I own. I told him a few, and he said, "I tried a business, but it didn't work, so I came back to insurance. What would you recommend I do?"

The Mindset of the Buyer:

I always say, 'I sell money; they sell houses.' When I make offers, I put in 20 and expect 19 rejections. But I only need one yes. I tell the agent, "Someone's getting my money this week. Either you or someone else." And I always put a 24–48-hour deadline. Pressure back on them. If the agent says, "We have three other buyers," I just smile and say, "Good luck. Call me if they pull out." I don't play their game. I create my own rules.

Ladders and Companies

People always say, "Climb the corporate ladder." I realised one day: why not build my own ladders? Companies are ladders. And other people can climb mine. I'm also scared of heights, so building ladders was safer than climbing them.

Key Takeaways

Start small (Coke cans) and learn to add zeros. -Replace liabilities (holidays, cars) with assets (vending machines, property). Read boring books that give you $400k solutions. -Buy smart, renovate smarter, and turn one house into multiple incomes. -Don't play by other people's rules; create your own. -Build ladders, don't climb them.

What Business Should I Start (or buy)?

Buying a McDonald's, KFC, or Subway is a proven way to make money. But let's be honest, those games usually belong to people with serious capital. They're not where you start; they're where you may end up. So where do you begin?

Start With What's in Your Hands

The first thing I usually say is, 'Look at the industry you're already in.' What skills are you learning? What contacts are you building? What gaps do you see every day? Most people undervalue this entirely. They think of their job as "just a wage." But I say:

Your boss is literally paying you to learn how to one day compete with them.

Example: Flooring

Say you work selling floating timber floorboards. Why not ask your boss or your existing customers if they'd also buy tiles, rubber flooring, or another complementary product from you?

Importing products from China (or anywhere else) isn't as hard as it used to be. The hard part is the contacts and trust. And you're already sitting on that goldmine while being paid to learn the trade.

See the Opportunity in Your Everyday

Just this Thursday, I had to call my insurance company. Someone reversed into my Porsche while I was eating sushi in Double Bay. No note, no details, just drove off. I was on the phone, and he was helping me with insurance issues, and he asked what type of business I own.

I told him a few, and he said, "I tried a business, but it didn't work, so I came back to insurance. He asked, "What would you recommend I do?"

I said, "Look at your own industry." - "You already know car insurance. You already have hundreds of client details. You know what they drive. You know what they pay."- "Why not start your own brokerage? You've got a ready-made customer base, and you can offer them a better deal."

He was shocked at how simple it sounded. But that's the point: most people look at the horizon and miss the gold lying at their feet. Don't Miss the People Right in Front of You

My brother is a successful man. He mentors pastors and church ministers. His heart is to help people expand their capacity and reach more lives, and that's a noble goal. He called me recently and asked, "What am I not seeing that could help me?" I said, "Sometimes you need to slow down in your busy life and talk to the Uber driver, the waitress, or the hostess on the plane." Here's the truth: a big vision is essential. - Big events and projects matter. - But too often we miss the small conversations, the hidden opportunities, the chance to bless someone, because we're rushing to the "grand scale."

Key Principle

The best business for you to start is not hidden in some faraway industry.

It's almost always in the contacts you already have, the skills you already know, and the problems you see every day.

Opportunities are often sitting right in front of us, but we're too busy looking for something shiny in the distance.

Real Estate – What Is the Best to Buy?

That depends on your specific situation. Self-storage units are one of the best real estate assets. However, they typically require a 40% deposit or investors to back you. That's not easy, but it's possible. The best returns I've ever seen are in retirement villages. But the red tape, regulations, and endless procedures make them a nightmare for me. It goes against what I value: time is my currency. For most beginners, I recommend residential real estate as a starting point. Especially dual-income properties, such as a house with a granny flat or a duplex. These typically generate enough rent to cover the mortgage and then some. That means you build cash flow, you achieve capital growth, and you create leverage to buy your next property using the equity. I am, and always will be, a fan of real estate because I can have control over it. I can buy it for a discount because I know how to, and I can also identify properties that I can generate dual or multiple incomes from. That might involve splitting the home into two and adding showers, toilets, etc.

I have shares and cryptocurrency, but I am not as fond of them as I am of property or businesses. People would argue and try to convince me that they can make certain returns, etc., but I see them as a gamble, and really, no one knows what a share will do unless you know Nancy Pelosi (US Senator). No one knows or has the control to influence them like I can with a business or property.

Unknown-Author

CHAPTER 6

THE EAGLE'S RENEWAL

An eagle can live up to seventy years. They are among the most determined of creatures. However, to reach that whole lifespan, something must happen around the age of forty.

By that time, the eagle's beak is blunt. Its claws are worn and can no longer be used for hunting. Its feathers are heavy, old, and limit its ability to fly. At this point, the eagle faces a choice: give up and die, or go through a painful process of renewal.

The eagle flies into the wilderness, where it begins breaking its own beak against a rock until it falls off. When the new beak grows in, it uses it to rip out its old claws. Then, one by one, it plucks away its feathers until it is bare and vulnerable.

This process takes about 150 days. It is brutal. It is painful. But in the end, the eagle emerges renewed, with a fresh beak, sharp claws, and strong new feathers. It can soar again. It is reborn for the second half of its life.

Do you want a new start, a fresh career in business?

We too face that kind of decision. Life presses us into moments where we cannot go on as we are. We must choose to endure a painful process of change if we want to live fully again.

If you've found yourself in a job that no longer fits, and you want to make changes, switch careers, or even start a business, it's good. This chapter is your map.

There is nothing like a new start, a new day, and a new season. Seasons and storms come and go; none are permanent. It's never too late to change. Colonel Sanders built KFC in his sixties. If he could turn fried chicken into a global franchise at that age, you and I can certainly start again.
So, let's get specific.

Two Proven Paths: New Business or New Position
Most readers sit in one of these two places:

- Start a business in the industry you already understand.

- Win a promotion (or a better role elsewhere) by proving you can grow revenue, not just "do your job."

Both paths use the same core truth: opportunity is usually right in front of you, not galaxies away.

Path A —Start a Business Where You Already Are

Whatever industry you're in, start there. Your unfair advantage is what you already know: the problems, the prices, the players, and the people.

Example (Insurance, think of any major insurer):

I just mentioned how I spoke with a man who left insurance to try another venture. It failed. He returned to an insurer, answering phones. I told him, "Why not consider a business already in your field? You have relationships. Use them, ethically and legally."

A Compliant Way to Leverage Your Network

This matters. Do not copy confidential client lists or breach employer policies. Instead:

- Become authorised (e.g., an Authorised Representative with a reputable brokerage).
- **Build a permission-based list:** connect on LinkedIn, ask contacts to opt in to your personal newsletter, share practical tips, and invite them to request quotes with their consent.
- **Specialise:** focus on one vertical (e.g., high-end car insurance for luxury vehicles, or trades- businesses).
- **Create a simple lead magnet:** "7 Ways to Cut Your Premium Without Cutting Cover." People exchange email for value.

Let's look at this with an example

$3,000 Micro-Launch Budget (example)

- Licensing/AR setup & basic compliance: $1,200–$1,500
- Domain, website, email, basic landing page: $300–$500
- Simple CRM + email platform (3–6 months): $150–$300
- LinkedIn Premium (3 months) + prospecting tool: $300–$450
- Minimal ads or printing (postcards to a tight niche): $250–$400
- Contingency: $200

(Tweak for your industry.)

Offer Ladder (keep it simple)

- **Free:** Coverage check-up + premium comparison (15 minutes).
- **Core:** Policy placement at market rates (your commission built in).
- **Upsells/Cross-sells:** Home & contents, life/TPD, business pack, tools & equipment.
- **Retention:** Annual review + claims advocacy.

Path B — Win a Promotion by Bringing a Plan

Let's say you're inside a big insurer and feel you've hit a ceiling.

Don't ask for a promotion; pitch a revenue project.

The Pitch: Sell More to Existing Customers

Conversion benchmarks

Existing customers: 60–70% probability of sale

New prospects: 5–20% probability

Why existing customers convert

Trust is already built.

Lower friction/education.

Easier upsell & cross-sell.

Relationship equity.

The "Luxury Vehicle Owner" Project (you can adapt this to any niche)

Identify a niche already in your book (e.g., owners of high-end vehicles).

Map adjacent policies they likely need (home, contents, life, business).

Build a 90-day pilot to increase the multi-policy attachment rate.

What you hand your manager:

One-Page Proposal (template)

- **Objective:** Lift policy-per-customer from 1.2 → 1.8 in 90 days among luxury vehicle clients.
- **Segment Size:** ~2,000 clients (example: use actual numbers).
- **Offer:** "Concierge Protection Review" — 20-minute bundled quote across auto + home + contents + life.
- **Process:** Email → phone follow-up → booked review; scripts included.
- **KPIs:** Contact rate, booked reviews, conversion rate, policies added, incremental premium, retention uplift.

- **Resources:** One senior underwriter for complex cases; one admin.
- **Compliance:** Customers opt in, provide recorded consent, and receive disclosures in accordance with policy.
- **Forecast:** See the simple model below.
- **Asks:** Pilot approval + named support + weekly stand-up.

Simple Pilot Model (illustrative)

2,000 contacts → 40% contactable = 800

800 contacted → 35% book review = 280

280 reviews → 55% add ≥1 policy = 154

Avg. added premium $1,200 → $184,800 new premium

Retention uplift on these customers +5–8% next renewal = long-tail value

Outcome either way: Even if leadership doesn't run with it, you've shown managerial thinking. Your name goes on the shortlist for senior sales roles, internally or at a competitor.

Mindset Shift: Don't "Do a Job." Build Revenue.

Most people wait for instructions. Leaders bring a plan. Set a standard for yourself: show up as the person who grows customers, not just answers calls. Dress the part. Be polite, helpful, and volunteer for work outside your current responsibilities. Opportunity notices momentum.

Practical Tools You Can Use Today

1) 10-Line Email to Former/Current Contacts (compliant, permission-based)

Subject: Quick protection check-up (15 mins)

Hi [Name],

I'm offering short, no-cost coverage check-ups for [niche, e.g., performance car owners] to help reduce premiums without compromising coverage.

If you'd like me to run a side-by-side comparison and highlight gaps, reply "YES" and I'll send a 3-question form and book a 15-minute slot.

No pressure if it's not better, we leave things as they are.

Cheers,

[Your Name]

[Licensing/AR details] | [Phone] | [Website]

2) 90-Day "Reborn Like an Eagle" Plan

- **Days 1–7 (Beak):** Decide your niche; write a one-page offer; set up basic tooling (domain, calendar, CRM).
- **Days 8–30 (Claws):** Contact 10–20 warm connections/day; post three educational tips/week; book reviews.
- **Days 31–60 (Feathers):** Deliver reviews; bundle additional policies/services; collect testimonials.
- **Days 61–90 (Flight):** Systemise: refine scripts, automate reminders, build a referral loop.

3) Mini Math for Your Book (plug-and-play)

- **Customer Ladder Value (CLV proxy):**

Average Annual Premium × Gross Margin × Retention Years

- **Attachment Gain:**

(Policies per Customer after − Policies per Customer before) × Avg Policy Margin × Customers in Segment

- **Resell Efficiency:**

Cost per Resell Lead ≈ 10–30% of Cost per New Lead (because lists + trust already exist)

A Word on Ethics & Law (protect yourself)

Don't export or use your employer's confidential data.

Build your own permission-based list.

Get licensed/authorised where required.

Use correct disclosures. Keep records of consent.

If leaving a role, honour non-solicitation and notice periods. This keeps your renewal season clean, today and ten years from now.

"It's not that I can't, how can I?"

Bring It Home

You don't need luck. You need a decision, a plan, and a first call.

Your 30-Minute Assignment (do it now):

Write your niche + offer in three lines.

Create a list of 20 individuals who could benefit and are legally eligible to be contacted.

Send the 10-line email to five of them.

Book two 15-minute reviews this week.

When an eagle renews, it does the brutal work in private, then it flies. Your turn.

P.S. If this chapter helps you land a role or launch a venture, email me your story. It might end up in the next book.

Is Borrowing Bad?

Yes and no. Smart borrowing to buy assets is how the wealthy grow their wealth. Bad borrowing to purchase toys is the most common way people stay broke. Surprisingly, bankruptcies don't usually come from low-income earners. They mostly come from white-collar professionals, because they have a higher capacity to borrow for liabilities. Liabilities make us poorer; Assets make us richer. It's that simple.

The "Luxury Trap"

Most professionals feel pressure to present themselves professionally. The BMW. The Mercedes. The big home with a pool. The European holiday. Designer bags and watches. Nothing wrong with any of that. I've got most of it myself (well, except for the pool and handbag). But here's the difference-I didn't borrow for them when I was young. I didn't spend my wage on them. I built assets first, and those assets now pay for my toys. When I see young guys in flash cars on finance, I can't help but think of those plastic hamster wheels. The mice run harder and harder, but get nowhere. That's what debt-for-toys is like: working harder just to stand still.

A Cabin paid for my Porsche

I always paid cash for cars, so they were just average. One day, I had $25k saved and was about to buy the best car I'd ever owned. But instead, I bought a cabin. I put it on-site at my storage units, rented it out, and the rental income pays for the loan on my Porsche. And the "night watchman" pays me to be there – I love it!!! So, I created an asset to buy my cars for the rest of my life. That idea wasn't planned. It hit me because I drove past a kit home company, saw the cabin, did a U-turn, and bought it. Sometimes opportunities come like that. You just have to be open enough to see them.

You Don't Always Need Money to Make Money

That old saying, "You need money to make money," is rubbish. Money can help, but creativity and trust are far more valuable. Take my self-storage units. I started with investors. Over the course of 5 years, I bought them all out one by one. Now I own them. Or my wine exporting business. One of the best businesses I've ever started. Cost me $0 upfront, and made up to $30,000 profit a month. How? I set up a deal where my supplier required a 30% deposit and a 70% balance due upon shipping. I gave my Chinese buyers the same terms, but at a marked-up price. That way, the cash flowed through me without costing me a cent, creativity over capital.

The Wine Story

Here's how it really started. One day, I was at a cafe in Sydney near the casino. I started chatting to a young couple, an Aussie guy and his Chinese girlfriend. I said hello in Chinese, and they were surprised I spoke a little. We swapped details.

The next day, I got a text from the girl asking to meet urgently. She broke down crying and told me her story: she'd lost $330k of investor money to a scammer who sold her a fake college. Out of desperation, she'd even sold herself to try and repay part of it. That day, she was planning to commit suicide, but messaged me as a last hope. I couldn't walk away. I got the scammer's details, organised a sit-down meeting, and found out people he knew that I knew, and encouraged him that his business and reputation meant more to him than a quick dollar, and mentioned his entire business and property were about to have a caveat put on them and dragged through court. I made it clear he was dealing with the wrong people. Long story short, he paid her back in full, and I was even shocked.

One of her Chinese investors flew over to meet me. They asked how much they owed me. I said, "Nothing. She was ripped off; it wasn't her fault." That simple act of kindness led to a sense of trust. And in China, trust is currency. They told me, "From now on, any business in Australia goes through you." That's how the wine business began. One connection. One act of helping someone for free. One bit of trust. And I'll never forget my saying:

"It costs nothing to be nice". But sometimes it pays more than you could ever plan."

Your Greatest Asset

Our biggest asset is our mind. That's why we need to learn, challenge, and create. Don't just accept what everyone says. Test ideas. Be curious. Break the status quo. Yes, take advice. But not everyone's opinion.

Notice this: the next time someone says, "If you want my opinion…" it's almost always a negative one. Rarely do they follow it with, "That's amazing, what a great idea!" So, filter opinions. Guard your thoughts. Fill your mind with knowledge, because your brain is your asset. Sharpen it daily.

Think of a sword. Left neglected, it rusts and weakens. But a sharp blade cuts through resistance. Your mind works the same way; the sharper it is, the faster you cut through problems. If your mind is dull, every obstacle feels like a wall. When your mind is sharp, every obstacle becomes a stepping stone.

Here's the truth: money can be taken, cars can break down, houses can burn down. But what you carry in your head, your skills, your knowledge, your ability to solve problems, that can never be stolen. That's why the wealthiest people on earth often started broke. They had nothing in their pockets, but wealth in their heads.

The "Why" Behind Wealth

Here's the real question: Why do you want money? A nice car? A big house? Sure, those are fun. But let me tell you, those things won't push you past your limits. They won't carry you through the tough seasons when nothing seems to work.

For me, the answer was simple: time.

The most essential thing in life is time. We all eventually run out of it. And most people trade away their best years for someone else's timetable. The alarm clock at 6. The traffic at 7. The boss at 9. The meeting at 11. The rush home at 6. And then it repeats. Week after week, year after year.

I didn't want to live like that. I set a mission: my time is not for sale.

I worked toward the point where no one could demand it, buy it, or control it. Only I decide who shares it. That, to me, is true freedom.

A Short Lesson

I once knew a man who worked sixty hours a week chasing promotions. He finally got the corner office, the title, and the salary. But when his son asked him to come watch his soccer game, the answer was always the same: "I can't, I've got work."

Years later, the boy stopped asking. The father had money, but missed the one thing money couldn't buy: time with his child.

That moment hit me. Wealth isn't what you own. Wealth belongs to those who control their hours.

CHAPTER 7

MY WAKE-UP CALL

When I was younger, I went down that same path. I traded hours for money, thinking that was the only way forward. At first, it felt normal to work hard, collect a wage, and climb the ladder. But deep down, I knew something was wrong.

One night, after a long shift, I sat in my car, exhausted. I realised I was building someone else's dream while my own life was slipping away. That thought shook me. I decided I would never again let another person own my hours.

It wasn't easy. It meant taking risks, building businesses, and making mistakes. But every step forward gave me more control. More choices. More time. And that was the reward I was chasing all along.

The Storage Units Story

I'll never forget one of my turning points. Back in the early 2000s, I purchased a block of land that everyone else considered useless. People shook their heads, told me it was a waste, said, "What are you doing? You'll lose your shirt."

But I saw something different. I saw potential. I knew self-storage was growing, and this land could become a valuable asset. I didn't have endless resources, but I had the asset that mattered most—my mind. I researched, I crunched numbers, and I took advice from those who had built before me.

Brick by brick, unit by unit, I transformed that land into a source of income. And here's the key: those storage units didn't just make money; they bought me time. Every unit rented was another piece of my freedom. Every door that rolled up was another reminder that my hours were no longer chained to someone else's desk.

That project taught me something powerful: wealth is built when you turn knowledge into action and create assets that give you back your most precious resource, time.

The Strata Maintenance Company Story

But freedom wasn't just about me. Once I had more control over my time, I started asking a bigger question: How can I use this freedom to help others?

That's when the Strata Maintenance Company was born. Initially, it was a straightforward cleaning, lawn, and maintenance service. However, I built it with a deeper purpose: to provide jobs and opportunities to people who would otherwise be overlooked. People with disabilities. People who'd struggled to find work. People who just needed someone to believe in them.

What started with a handful of sites grew into hundreds. Vans on the road, staff in uniforms, people proud to say they had work they could depend on.

And here's what I realised: the same freedom I wanted for myself, control over my own time, was precisely what I was giving to them. When someone who has been told they'll never make it suddenly has a steady job, income, and a future... that's real wealth. That's impact.

The Strata Maintenance Company wasn't just a business. It was a way of proving that wealth is not just measured in dollars, but in the lives changed along the way.

Your Turn

So, let me ask you: if money were no object, how would you spend your time?

With family? Creating? Exploring? Helping others? Building something that outlives you?

Your answer to that question is your real "why." It's the fuel that will drive you when the road gets hard.

Because money without a mission is wasted.

But money with a purpose makes you unstoppable.

How I Bought My Time

You don't need to be a millionaire to buy back your time. You just need to cover your life expenses humbly, diligently, and without competing with anyone else's lifestyle. Here's the maths: Say you need $1500/week to live-

That's $300 per day across a five-day working week. Each asset you build is like buying back one of those days. For me, the first step was creating a granny flat on my dad's property. That single move gave me $ 1,120 per month. It paid for my Fridays. I literally repurchased my Fridays. Next goal: Thursdays. Then Wednesdays, etc. Over time, through real estate, storage units, and businesses, everything I had accumulated, I practically owned. That's when I stopped working for a wage.

Two Keys to Buying Time

Increase your income – Create assets that generate a monthly income. Even small ones stack up. Reduce your liabilities – Don't tie yourself to loans for unnecessary expenses; cut the things you don't need. Yes, I love toys. Cars, holidays, watches. But I refused to give up my time for them. First, I bought my time with assets. Then, those assets bought the toys for me.

The Truth About Time

Time is more precious than anything you can buy. If I could trade everything I own for more time, I would. There's even an old proverb that says: "Honour your mother and father, and you will live a long life." That's the only thing I've ever read that connects directly to living longer. So don't waste time. Please don't sell it cheaply. Don't trade it for a toy. Your days are your true wealth; repurchase them one by one.

This chapter serves as the anchor to the entire book. Trying to make sense of all the stories: the Coke cans, the vending machines, the cabins, the Porsche, the wine deal. All of it points back to one theme: Use your brain to create assets. Use your assets to buy your time. Once you own your time, everything else becomes possible.

CHAPTER 8

THE WEEKEND MILLIONAIRE

During this time, I refused to take out a loan for a car, pool, or a bigger home, because in my mind, that meant selling back my Wednesday or Thursday. Every loan I applied for required me to buy an asset that would help me afford a day off work. Now, let me tell you about the guys who do the opposite. It's hilarious, and you can spot them a mile away.

I call them the Weekend Millionaires. You'll see them in Sydney clubs- always in a group, never solo, spending $800 for a private booth. Fake Rolex glints in the neon lights; Gucci belt buckles shine like lighthouses. (BALI gift). A $500 bottle of vodka that the club owner bought for $50 at Dan Murphy's. A couple of mixers thrown in for good measure. Then come the 22-year-old girls. They're smart, they'll sit, smile, and sip just long enough to get three free drinks... then leave before anything is expected. The "W.E. millionaires" panic, drop another $500 on another bottle, and try again. By now, they need to impress with a bit of white powder, because without it, the older girls (24, haha) won't hang around for long. Sunday comes, cash is gone, but they still need to be seen. So, they grab a cafe table by the beach, order one entree and one drink, and stretch it out for two hours just to look the part.

Then Monday hits, flat broke. But by Friday night, they're back on the treadmill. It's both comical and tragic. These guys are selling back their Fridays, Saturdays, and Sundays just to look cool for a few hours. Meanwhile, I'd rather drive an average car and keep my Wednesdays. And here's the thing: money won't solve your problems. It won't fix you. It will only magnify who you already are. If you're insecure, broke, or having money, and your thinking is precisely the same, just with fancier receipts. The Weekend Millionaire looks rich - Asset Builders are!

How to Make Good Decisions

Often in life, we watch someone make a choice that propels them forward. From the outside, it can look like luck or genius, and we think,

"Wow, what a brilliant move, I wish I had done that." Other times, we notice people who seem to make good choices, one after another, consistently, and it leaves us wondering: "How do they do it? What's their secret?" The truth is, good choices don't come from luck. They come from principles, focus, and a pattern of supporting the original decision with the right actions that follow.

Probe Deeper — Don't Just Settle

Don't settle for what looks good; probe for what is actually good. There's a big difference. Sometimes life doesn't hand you a spotlight showing the whole path ahead. Instead, you just get a lamp for your feet. As the scripture says: "Your word is a lamp unto my feet." A lamp doesn't light up the whole street; it just gives enough light to take the next step. That's how good choices are made. Step by step. Keep moving forward with the light you have.

Focus Like a Magnifying Glass

Here's something I drilled into my son so much that he tattooed it on his arm:

"Don't chase two rabbits."

If you do, you'll miss both. Focus on one at a time. This principle changes everything. Life is like using a magnifying glass; it can make things bigger, but if it's held steady at the proper distance, it doesn't just show focus; it creates fire. Good decisions often come down to this: focus long enough for the solution to become apparent.

It's Not Just the Choice — It's What Comes After

Rash, emotional, or rushed choices rarely lead to greatness. But here's the key: even when you make a good choice, it's the actions that follow that determine whether it becomes a brilliant one.

Think of dating. At first, anyone can seem nice. If six months later it doesn't work out, you might call it a bad choice. But was it really? Or was it that the choices you made after the first one didn't support the original decision? If you date with the mindset: I'm just dating until I find someone I genuinely want to marry and commit my life to, then when you do find that person, all your choices that follow will align with that commitment. That's what cements the original choice and makes it good.

But if you start to hedge your bets, staying in the relationship while being open to meeting someone "better" than every decision you make will erode the foundation of your first choice. Over time, the original choice collapses. This principle applies everywhere, not just in relationships. Business. Friendships. Money. Health. The original choice might have been fine, but inconsistent follow-up choices weaken it until it breaks.

The Secret Behind "Smart" People

So, when you see people who seem smart, wise, or lucky with their decisions, it's often not that their first choice was perfect. It's that they aligned every other choice with it. They didn't contradict themselves, they didn't waver, and they stayed committed long enough for the fire to come. That's the difference between a one-off good decision and a life of consistently good choices.

The Danger of Double-Mindedness. I remember once having a conversation with someone I was dating. She told me about her girlfriend, who was married, but while on holiday, she met another man. She said she "fell in love" with him, got divorced, and eventually married him. Then she said to me, "See, it was meant to be." I pushed back. I said, "No, I don't believe that's right. If someone is married, they shouldn't even be open to meeting someone else. They should be single-minded about being married, not chasing someone better looking, richer, or more exciting." To me, that kind of openness isn't freedom, it's instability. And it made sense why the woman telling me this story was divorced herself.

The truth is simple: don't get married if you still want to play the dating game. Stay single. Have fun. But don't pretend you've committed if your choices don't align with it. It isn't always about making the perfect choice the first time. However, it always matters that your following decisions align with the original one. Otherwise, you sabotage yourself. Like the old line says: "A double-minded person is unstable in all their ways."

Making Good Choices in Life and Business

If a young person came and asked me, "Is it a good idea to become a carpenter?" most of us would probably say yes. It's a solid trade, steady income, and plenty of work. We'd encourage him to consider an apprenticeship, pursue further education, work for a reputable company, and commit to learning the trade. But notice something: we wouldn't also say, "Great, and while you're at it, do plumbing and painting too." No, because focus matters. When someone is committed to their craft, we know they'll succeed. The same goes for life choices. And here's the truth: failing at a task, career, or business doesn't mean you are a failure. It simply means that at that time, due to a lack of knowledge, timing, money, or even the economy, you failed. That's time and chance, not identity.

Do Your Homework

When I need to make a decision, I conduct thorough research. The more informed I am, the more confident and calculated my choice will be. That doesn't mean I'll avoid all pain, but it minimises unnecessary pain. I live by

"It's not 'I can't' but 'how can I?'" Every problem has a solution. The question is, are you going to be the one creative enough to find it? Why not? You're unique. No one else has your exact mix of mistakes, lessons, experiences, or network. Hidden inside that is the solution that only you can bring. For me, I ask two questions before committing: Do I really want this? Am I willing to invest the time and resources necessary to find the solution? If the answer is yes, I lean in. If I'm half-hearted, I move on. I like simple things, not easy, but straightforward. If I can't see the "why" or the "how," I don't waste energy chasing it.

A Framework for Good Decisions

So, how do you know if a choice is a good one? Here's a practical test: Check your motive. Why am I making this choice? If the reason is fear, ego, or short-term comfort, be cautious. If it's growth, integrity, or long-term benefit, you're on firmer ground. Test it against your values. Would you still make this choice if no one knew about it? If it breaks your core principles, it's probably not a good choice, no matter the payoff. Do the "future-you" test. Imagine yourself one year from now, looking back. Will you thank yourself or regret it?

Consider best- and worst-case scenarios. If the worst-case scenario is survivable and the best-case scenario is worthwhile, the risk is reasonable. If the downside could destroy what matters most, rethink it. Seek disinterested wisdom. Ask someone you trust who doesn't have a stake in the outcome. They'll see blind spots you miss. This way, choices stop being shots in the dark and start becoming stepping stones. Even when they don't pan out, you can walk away knowing you made the best decision you could with the knowledge, values, and foresight you had. That alone is success.

All these topics relate to my goal of becoming a time billionaire - what I buy must generate passive income and profit, and I must negotiate to get the best deal. Hence, it is feasible and practical to make something into an asset. Being single-minded, not trying to look like a weekend millionaire, and delaying my goal are not the right approaches. Instead, I should purposefully make informed choices, conduct research, and acquire the necessary knowledge to make these decisions. These choices are connected to the puzzle.

CHAPTER 9

RELATIONSHIPS

Relationships can mean a lot of things- family, a lover, friendships, business, or even casual mates. They all have a place in our lives. Some will last a lifetime, some a few years, and others just a season. And there's nothing wrong with any of them. Sadly, some end badly, especially relationships with lovers, but sometimes even with family or close friends. Over the years, I've had many mates who felt like best friends for a season, and many are still good friends now. Life has seasons: single, not busy, flat-out busy, and new babies; it all changes the dynamic.

But those friendships are essential. They keep us sane. It's great just having someone to hang out with on weekends, or to call and say, "Mate, I just met this gorgeous girl!" And then you realise she looks fantastic, as long as she doesn't smile because half her teeth are missing, or she's got the most beautiful hair, as long as she's wearing her wig. But you know what I mean. It's about sharing the highs and lows of life. I remember when I won a multi-million-dollar contract, I went out with two friends and we celebrated. They were genuinely happy for me. And I remember when one of my most loyal long-term friends, Matt, tried for twelve years to have a child. When he finally got the news, it was happening, we celebrated with a fat cigar and dinner. He was a non-drinker, a church pastor, so that cigar was about the naughtiest thing he'd ever do. Relationships make those moments matter.

Building Strong Relationships.

Choose connection over being right -Winning an argument but losing the relationship is a hollow victory. Sometimes the most powerful words you can say are: "I see your point" or simply, "I'm sorry." Listen to understand, not just to reload- Some people don't really listen, they just wait for their turn to talk. (I've mentioned this before, but it's one of my biggest pet hates.) If you can really hear what's underneath someone's words, you'll often solve a problem before it even begins.

Develop a Genuine Interest in Others

Listen actively: Pay attention to what others say without just waiting to speak. - Ask questions: Be curious about people's goals, challenges, and passions. - Remember details: Personal touches (e.g., remembering names, birthdays, or interests) go a long way. Tip: Read "How to Win Friends and Influence People" by Dale Carnegie, for timeless wisdom on this.

Offer Value First

Don't approach relationships with a "what can I get" mindset. - Look for ways to help, connect, or support others without expecting immediate returns.

Examples:

Share helpful resources or articles. - Make introductions between people who could help each other- Offer your expertise when appropriate.

Communicate Clearly and Consistently

Be responsive. Timely replies build trust and reliability. - Be transparent. Say what you mean and mean what you say- Don't disappear when things get tough, that's when relationships are tested.

Build Trust Over Time

Keep your promises. - Own your mistakes. - Stay consistent in your values and actions.

Trust isn't built overnight; it's built by showing up, again and again, with integrity.

Develop Strategically (but authentically)

Attend events, join communities, and attend conferences, but focus on quality, not quantity.

Focus on building deep connections with a few people rather than shallow ones with many.

Follow up after events with a quick message or LinkedIn connection, referencing your conversation.

Maintain Relationships, Don't Just Start Them

Check in periodically, not just when you need something. Share wins and updates, but also ask about the other person's well-being. Celebrate others' successes.

Small gestures over time compound into strong bonds.

Stay Professional and Respect Boundaries

Respect others' time, space, and communication preferences. - Avoid gossip, venting, or oversharing in professional settings. Be emotionally intelligent: read the room, understand different perspectives, and manage your reactions effectively.

Keep Learning and Growing

The more valuable and self-aware you are, the more you attract quality relationships.

Work on your skills, mindset, and leadership abilities.

Final Thought:

Relationships in business and careers are like investments; the earlier and more consistently you invest, the greater the returns over time.

CHAPTER 10

BOUNDARIES ARE NOT WALLS.

Boundaries protect us and keep us on the right path. Walls block connections. A boundary helps you run your race without crashing into someone else's lane. A wall just shuts everyone out. Sometimes, a wall is necessary, but knowing the difference is crucial. Saying "no" when needed actually builds respect. And never underestimate the power of a genuine friend with integrity asking you how you really are.

When most people hear the word boundaries, they immediately imagine something rigid and impenetrable, like a fortress wall built to keep others out. But in truth, boundaries are not walls. Boundaries are not about isolation, punishment, or shutting people down; they are about setting clear expectations and maintaining healthy relationships. They are centered on clarity, respect, and fostering sustainable conditions for growth, both personally and professionally.

Think of a boundary less like a brick wall and more like a property line. A property line makes it clear where your space begins and ends, but it doesn't prevent you from opening the gate to invite someone in. It simply communicates ownership, responsibility, and respect. Without property lines, confusion reigns: people don't know where they can walk, park, or build. Boundaries in business work similarly.

Boundaries Define, Walls Confine

Walls are built out of fear. They are meant to keep people at a distance and protect them from perceived harm. Boundaries, on the other hand, are created out of self-respect. They allow you to interact with others while still preserving your energy, focus, and integrity.

A wall says, "Stay away. I don't trust you."

A boundary says, "Here's how I can engage with you in a healthy, productive way."

In business, a wall might look like refusing to delegate tasks because "no one else can do it right." A boundary looks like training your team, setting clear expectations, and holding them accountable while trusting them to do their part. One isolates; the other empowers.

Boundaries Signal Respect

One of the greatest misconceptions is that boundaries are selfish. In fact, they are the opposite. Boundaries make relationships, whether with clients, employees, or partners, healthier because they clarify what each side can expect.

If you don't set clear working hours, a client may email you at midnight and expect a response. That's not their fault; it's yours for not communicating your limits.

If you don't outline payment terms, you may end up resenting a customer who pays late, even though you never drew a line in the first place.

Boundaries are a sign that you respect your own time, energy, and expertise, and by extension, you respect others enough to let them know where you stand.

Boundaries Create Freedom

It may seem paradoxical, but boundaries create more freedom, not less. Imagine driving without traffic lights or lanes. Everyone would be free to do as they please, but chaos would make movement impossible. Boundaries are the lines on the road of business and life. They allow flow, speed, and safety. When you set boundaries, you:

- Save your energy for the most critical priorities.
- Reduce conflict by eliminating unspoken assumptions.
- Empower others by showing them what is and isn't theirs to handle.

The absence of boundaries doesn't create freedom; it creates burnout. The presence of boundaries allows for a clear focus on what matters most.

Boundaries Require Courage

Setting boundaries is uncomfortable because it requires you to communicate directly. It's easier to avoid a challenging conversation, agree to everything, and then secretly resent it later. However, that avoidance always comes at a higher cost in the long run.

Leaders who master boundaries become models of clarity. They show that it's possible to say "no" without guilt, to negotiate without hostility, and to enforce agreements without shame. This courage creates stronger teams and healthier businesses.

Practical Ways to Set Boundaries Without Building Walls

Communicate early, not after a problem arises. Don't wait until you're frustrated; set expectations up front.

Be specific. "I need more respect" is a vague statement. "I don't take calls after 6 PM" is clear.

Stay consistent. A boundary you enforce only sometimes isn't a boundary at all.

Allow flexibility where appropriate. A property line can include a gate. Boundaries should allow for space for trust, collaboration, and exceptions to be made consciously.

Model respect for others' boundaries. If you expect your clients to respect your time, respect theirs as well.

Boundaries are not walls; they are bridges of understanding. They allow you to stay connected without being consumed, to give without being drained, and to grow without being overrun. In business and in life, learning to set boundaries is not about keeping people out; it's about maintaining a healthy balance. It is about letting the right people in, under the right conditions, so that both sides can thrive.

Keys to Building Strong Relationships

Consistency builds trust faster than grand gestures.

A little daily care outshines one big romantic or friendly act followed by neglect. People love a nice dinner, but they tend to forget about it eventually. What they won't forget is the one time you didn't show up. I've had to learn this the hard way. I used to forget birthdays, coffee catch-ups, or meetings, and I've lost friendships over it. I've had to beg forgiveness and tell the truth: "Mate, I just forgot." And as much as I hate to admit it, forgetting does show that maybe we weren't as excited or didn't care as much as we should have. Brutal but partly true. These days, I use my calendar like a lifeline, because consistency matters.

Ask yourself: "Am I giving what I want to receive?" Love, respect, patience, encouragement, whatever you want more of, start by giving it first. Don't keep score. Don't look for a payday. Just be it.

This one changed my life. When you consistently give authentic encouragement, it eventually shines through the falseness and masks people put on. But here's the catch: it takes patience. Most give up too quickly. They think, "I've been kind for weeks and it's not coming back to me." But absolute consistency wins over time. I've hurt people in my past, and sometimes they've cut me off completely. You can't always fix it. But you can choose not to repeat the same mistake with the next relationship.

Let people change

The version of someone you met five or ten years ago is not who they are now. If you freeze them in their old self, you kill the relationship's growth. I can testify to this myself. Ten years ago, I was heavier, more opinionated, and never danced; my ex-wife of 28 years never once saw me dance. I thought it was "soft" or weird. Now I love dancing more than anyone I know. I've even learned a little salsa (not bad for a bloke from south-west Sydney!). At first, I had female friends help me out, and once I stopped caring what I looked like, I just got better. These days, I even rate myself when I hit the dance floor.

Lesson? People evolve. Please give them the space to. Sometimes the best teaching isn't telling people what to do every five minutes; it's showing them how to live with humility.

Learn each other's "currency"

Everyone has their own love language: words of affirmation, quality time, gifts, acts of service, or physical touch. Speak theirs, not yours. I didn't get this when I was younger. I just gave what I thought was love or respect in my language. I like words of affirmation and physical touch, but that doesn't work with someone who wants acts of service. People need to receive it in their own love language. Learn their "currency." It takes effort, but the rewards are enormous.

Handle small cracks before they become canyons.

Resentment = unspoken disappointment over time. If you don't deal with issues, they grow like cancer. I've learned this in my own relationship. I've said to my partners in the past, You can disagree with me, just do it with love and kindness. Softly." Because here's the truth: most men (myself included) don't hear a thing when we're being yelled at. We put on invisible headphones and that one famous song only men hear -comes on: "Blah blah blah, blah blah blah."

If you deal with things quickly and with kindness, they don't become significant issues. Leave them to fester, and they can wreck everything.

In Business, Never Sacrifice Integrity for a Quick Win

You can recover money. You rarely recover a damaged reputation. And news travels fast, terrible news. Negative news spreads with passion, momentum, and exaggeration. Protect your name. Integrity always outlives a deal. People Won't Remember Every Word You Say... But They Always Remember How You Made Them Feel. I touched on this earlier, but here's one thing I do strategically and also very genuinely: when I first meet someone, I like to give a compliment. It doesn't matter if it's their shoes, their energy, their laugh, or their work, anything. People may forget what I said, but they never forget how I made them feel at that moment. Now let's go a little deeper. Let's see if I can use some big words like "wheelbarrow" and impress you.

The Heart Before the Brain

When we think of intelligence, most of us immediately picture the brain, the control centre, the seat of logic, the organ we associate with success. Yet, long before the brain even begins to take shape, another organ makes its entrance: the heart.

Biologically, in human embryonic development, the heart begins to form and beat before the brain is fully developed. The heart doesn't wait for neural networks to instruct it; it establishes its rhythm, initiates circulation, and sustains life while the brain is still in its earliest stages. This simple fact carries a profound message: the heart is not dependent on the brain; it precedes it.

Unknown-Author

The Primacy of the Heart

The heart's early formation reminds us that life itself is first driven by rhythm, connection, and flow, not by thought, strategy, or calculation. The heart sustains the embryo, circulating nutrients and oxygen, laying the foundation for all future growth. Without the heart's independent function, the brain would never develop.

In this way, the heart is both literal and symbolic, serving as a guiding force.

Independence,

To say the heart is independent of the brain is not to deny the value of intellect. The heart and brain eventually become deeply interconnected, with vast networks of nerves linking them in constant communication. But independence means that the heart has its own intelligence, its own authority, and its own way of perceiving the world.

Modern science even supports this idea. The heart contains an intricate nervous system, sometimes referred to as the "heart brain," capable of sensing, learning, and remembering. The heart sends more signals to the brain than the brain sends to the heart. In other words, our thoughts are shaped as much by the heart as the heart is by our thoughts.

Leading From the Heart

In business and leadership, this truth carries weight. Too often, decisions are made purely from the head, analysing numbers, projecting outcomes, and calculating risks. While these skills are necessary, they are incomplete. Without the wisdom of the heart, decisions risk being cold, transactional, or disconnected from human values.

The leaders who inspire us most are not just thinkers; they are feelers. They act with empathy, intuition, and courage. They recognise that success is not measured only by profit margins but also by impact, legacy, and the well-being of people.

The brain asks, "What will this cost?"

The heart asks, "What will this create?"

The brain weighs the risks.

The heart feels the possibilities.

Together, they form a balance. But the heart must not be silenced, because it was here first.

The Heart is a Compass

When facing difficult decisions, it's common to experience conflict between the head and the heart. Logic may argue in one direction, while intuition points in another. In these moments, it helps to remember that the heart is not a secondary opinion; it is the original voice.

The heart is a compass. It doesn't always speak in spreadsheets or statistics. It says in resonance, in alignment, in the quiet sense of this feels right or this feels wrong. Ignoring that voice often leads to regret. Honouring it, even when difficult, builds authenticity and trust.

Practical Applications

Check in with your heart before big decisions. Ask not only, "Does this make sense?" but also, "Does this feel right?"

Use logic to refine, not override. The brain can test and structure the insights the heart provides.

Cultivate heart intelligence. Practices like mindfulness, gratitude, and deep listening strengthen your ability to access your heart's wisdom.

Lead with empathy. People remember how you made them feel long after they forget what you said.

Closing Thought

The fact that the heart forms before the brain is not just a detail of biology; it is a blueprint for how to live and lead. The heart comes first, both in terms of time and importance. It carries its own wisdom, its own independence, and its own rhythm. The brain is a brilliant strategist, but the heart is the original leader.

When you allow the heart to lead and the brain to serve, you honour the design of life itself.

CHAPTER 11

GUARDING YOUR HEART -RENEWING YOUR MIND

Science tells us our brain controls our body, but the heart is far more potent than we give it credit for. In 1991, scientists discovered over 40,000 cells in the heart, arranged in a manner that creates a neural network, similar to those in the brain, but distinct from them. These sensory neurites can actually think, feel, and remember. That means trauma isn't just stored in your brain; it can also live in your heart. You may process something logically in your mind, but until it's dealt with in your heart, it lingers.

Even before science, ancient wisdom knew this. Proverbs says, "Above all else, guard your heart." Interesting. Thousands of years ago, people already understood the deeper reality: the heart drives who we are.

Our brain can be renewed by filling it with positive, truthful, and uplifting information. But the heart must be guarded. Because it's the heart that pushes us, steers us, and exposes who we really are. Fear, love, courage, despair, these all flow from the heart. We can't think ourselves into loving someone. We just do or we just don't. I take this seriously. I try not to let people's actions, the economy, or even life's chaos dictate what's in my heart. I renew my mind, yes, but I protect my heart.

The Heart Behind the Mask.

The Disturbing Pleasure in Pain

One of the darkest parts of human behaviour is when someone gets pleasure out of another person's unwarranted pain. I listen to a great thinker and word warrior, Jordan Peterson, he discussed this, and it always resonates with me deeply. I've seen glimpses of this in people before. And I'll be honest: it unsettles me. Even if I don't like someone, when something bad happens to them, I don't take pleasure in it. It might make sense that specific actions carry certain outcomes, "you reap what you sow," but that's very different from enjoying another person's downfall. When this behaviour is at its worst, it shows up in a small percentage of society, the five percent we call psychopaths, sociopaths, or sadists. I'm not saying everyone who laughs at someone else's pain is a psychopath. But when you start to taste pleasure in unwarranted suffering, you're drifting into dangerous territory. That kind of trait corrodes relationships, reputations, and ultimately, the soul. The truth is, this is a heart issue. Often, those who enjoy the pain of others are carrying pain themselves. They feel, "I suffered unfairly, so you should too." It's a poisoned way of living.

The Healthy Opposite

The healthy heart does the opposite: it rejoices when others get a win, even if they didn't "deserve" it. Someone says, "I can't believe I got this opportunity; I just got lucky." The generous-hearted person smiles and says, "That's fantastic, I'm happy for you." That is the kind of spirit that builds strong friendships, strong marriages, and strong communities.

Motives That Glow in the Dark

Today, I spoke with my younger son, a brilliant and stimulating conversationalist. He said something that stuck with me: "Sometimes people do things that seem fine on the surface, but you can just tell their motivation isn't right." He's spot on. You see it when someone gives a speech: are they doing it to genuinely add value, or simply to bask in attention and reverence?

At a distance, you might not notice. But get closer, and their true motives glow in the dark. The same thing happens online. I laugh when I see someone post a selfie, front and centre, with a friend blurred in the background, and the caption reads: "Humbled to be standing beside my great friend, happy birthday!" Let's be real: there's nothing "humble" about that. I take selfies too, but when I do, I call it what it is: showing off, having fun, teasing a little. What I won't do is pretend my showing off is humility. People prefer honesty over fake dribble.

The Wrong Picture

Here's the problem: when we're young, we absorb ideas about what life should look like. Those ideas paint a picture of who we think we should be. However, if the original picture is off, everything we add to it, the frames, the decorations, will also be off. That's why so many people keep walking further down the wrong path. Being lost doesn't bother them, because they don't even know they're lost. But if you feel lost? If you feel empty? Don't panic. That's a good sign. At least you know. Awareness is the first step to turning back, finding the right path, and painting the picture you were meant to live out.

Building a Life That Lasts

Why am I bringing this up in a book about money, real estate, and relationships? Because your heart attitude will make or break everything else. If you want to build wealth, foster strong relationships, and create a life that leaves a lasting legacy, you must start here. A cruel or selfish heart will sabotage your future. A kind and generous heart will build it.

The Bus Driver Lesson

I remember when my son was ten, he said, "Dad, I want to be a bus driver when I grow up." I loved it. It was such an innocent and thoughtful dream to drive people around, to serve, to be part of their day. I smiled and said, "Son, that's great. But why not also think about owning the bus business?" I wasn't mocking him. I would have been proud if he had become a bus driver. It was about expanding his vision, helping him see the bigger opportunities life has to offer. And that's the point. I'm not against jobs. I respect good employees. I employ them myself! But I want people to know they can be more if they choose. Working at a cafe or bar isn't wrong. Driving buses isn't bad. But life is easier when you add assets instead of piling up liabilities. It puts less pressure on marriages, it gives you choices, and it frees you up to live generously. Who knows? Maybe the next billionaire is reading this right now. Why not? It could be you.

Anxiety and Gratitude

Here's a fascinating study I came across: the same part of the brain that fuels anxiety is also responsible for gratitude. And it can't do both at once. - Think about what King Solomon said, "Don't be anxious, but in everything give thanks." Maybe he knew something about us, and how our minds work. So, if you're anxious, try this: start listing things you're thankful for. Your health. Family. Friends. A roof over your head. A good laugh. Even something as small as your morning coffee. Gratefulness forces anxiety to take a back seat.

A Baby's First Language

Here's a thought: before a baby learns English (or any language), what language do they think in? Maybe it's not words at all. Perhaps it's that "heart-brain" language, feelings, impressions, intuition. Something deeper than speech.

How should we deal with arguments?

Another proverb says: "There is a way that seems right to a man, but in the end, it leads to death."

I take this to mean that people aren't always jerks. Sometimes they genuinely think they're right, but they're actually way off track. That's why, when I argue or disagree with someone, I remind myself that they may not be trying to be a jerk, but they genuinely believe they are right. So, when I argue, I try to keep in mind that they are not being disagreeable; they believe they are right, but they are totally the opposite. The turning point for me came when I re-read it about two years later- what if ...I'm the one who seems right, and in fact, it's leading me to death / totally wrong? Wow! This made me think.

This one shift has transformed my relationships. I argue less. I listen more. And I don't look like such a jerk myself. (Though for the record, I still have plenty of jerks as friends. Hahaha.) It's a principle I'll live by for the rest of my life. No one is right all the time, but often we are convinced we are right and they are wrong, but take this on board and you will transform your conversations! And a tip – underline this section and leave the book open for your partner to read it accidentally :))

Living in the Present

If you're angry, you're living in the past. If you're fearful, you're living in the future. If you're at peace, you're living in the present. That one thought alone can re-frame your entire day. I read that about 80% of the things we worry about never actually happen. Let that sink in, four out of five of your worries are fairy tales - Tinkerbell owns them. They're just clutter, wasting mental space, stealing joy, and keeping you from being present. When I was younger, someone asked me sarcastically, "Have you ever worried so much that it actually fixed the problem?" That hit me hard. The answer was obvious. Worrying fixes nothing, except maybe adding a few more wrinkles to your forehead. That simple moment changed how I thought about fear and worry. Now, I try to live by this: my best days are ahead of me, not behind me. I don't want to live stuck in yesterday's regrets or tomorrow's fears. I want to live today- alive, thankful, able to enjoy the moment. I often say this to myself and my friends, "Who knows, today could be the most fantastic day of your life? Who knows, one day has to be. Maybe it's your best week-month. Every morning, ask yourself and your partner – today could be the best day of our lives- it's not hype or fake, it's a statement that could be true! I know that when I'm expecting-hoping for something, my eyes are open a little wider and my ears are open to an idea.

Sand- Pearl or Problem? -Think of sand in your eye, it's an irritant. But in an oyster, it becomes a pearl: same material, different outcome. Irritations reveal who we are. Do they turn us bitter, or better? Pearl, or problem? Don't allow problems and issues to wreck your day -open your eyes and see the opportunities that might come along.

Be Careful with Your Thinking

Thinking becomes words, Words become actions, Actions become habits, Habits become your future. Guard your thoughts, because they're building your life whether you realise it or not. Imagine how much lighter we'd all live if we stopped carrying everyone else's opinions around like a backpack of bricks. Remember, except for your closest circle, most are just passing through life.

This chain reaction begins quietly, often unnoticed, in the privacy of your own mind. The thoughts you entertain today are laying the bricks of the life you'll walk in tomorrow.

The Weight of Thought

I love the saying: "Small minds make small things big. Big minds make big things trivial."

If your thinking is small, you magnify problems, take offence easily, and give energy to distractions. But when you're thinking expands, you gain perspective. You stop sweating the small stuff and focus instead on vision, growth, and making a meaningful contribution.

Another truth that set me free: "It's none of your business what others think."

How many opportunities have been lost because we worried too much about opinions? Imagine how much lighter your life would feel if you stopped carrying other people's judgements like a backpack full of bricks. Most of those opinions belong to people who aren't even walking your path. Other than your tight circle, the people who know you deeply, most others are just visitors passing through. Their commentary is background noise, not direction.

Thoughts are Architecture

Your thinking is not random; it's architectural. Every thought is either constructing or demolishing something in your future.

Negative, self-defeating thoughts lay shaky foundations.

Worry and comparison are like termites that eat away at stability.

Positive, disciplined thoughts lay bricks of confidence, resilience, and possibility.

To change your results, you must first change your thinking. The mind is the workshop where the blueprint of your life is drawn.

Guarding the Gates

Since thoughts are so powerful, you must become the gatekeeper of your mind.

Watch your inputs. What you read, watch, and listen to feeds your thinking garbage in, garbage out, greatness in, greatness out.

Challenge your inner critic. Every time a thought says, "I can't," ask, "Who says?"

Speak what you want to see. Words are thoughts amplified. When you speak possibility, you build momentum.

Surround yourself wisely. Your circle influences your thought patterns. Choose people who expand your mind, not shrink it.

Think the Future

Your future does not just arrive; it is shaped. And the raw material of that future is your thinking.

- Think scarcity, and you will see limits everywhere.
- Think abundance, and you will see opportunities.
- Think resentment, and you will live in chains.
- Think gratitude, and you will walk in freedom.

Your thoughts are either anchors or sails. Anchors hold you down. Sails move you forward. The choice is yours every day.

Closing Reflection

Be careful with your thinking, not because it's fragile, but because it's powerful. Your thoughts are architects of your destiny, whether you realise it or not. Protect them. Feed them wisely. Aim them toward what matters most.

Because in the end, you don't just live the life you want, you live the life you think.

CHAPTER 12

THE BRAIN'S SECRET WEAPON

Our minds are influential, more influential than we usually give them credit for. Neuroscientists talk about neuroplasticity (yes, I had to cut and paste that word, too). Fifteen letters in that word, I give up after 6/7 -Here's the wild part: every time you imagine doing something in vivid detail, your brain rewires itself, as if you'd actually done it. If you mentally rehearse shooting basketballs, playing piano, or giving a speech, with real sensory detail (the sound of the ball, the weight of the keys, the feel of the microphone), your brain strengthens the same pathways as physical practice. That's why elite athletes, top performers, and successful entrepreneurs use mental rehearsal. It's free, risk-free practice that stacks the odds in your favour. Your brain doesn't perfectly distinguish between what's real and what's vividly imagined. In other words, you can literally train your future in your imagination. Have you heard that saying - it's all in your imagination! Well, it actually is! Who would have thought that an intended backhand comment would turn out to be highly intelligent?

Suckers Game -Trading Time for Money

Work for Assets, Not Just Money

Most people wake up every day and go to work for one primary purpose: to earn a living. The paycheck becomes the end goal. However, the wealthy mindset flips this: you don't work for money; you work to build assets that continue to produce money, whether you're working or not. Your boss isn't just paying you for Labour. He's training you in his system. Every skill you acquire is a future tool to build your own assets. In many ways, your boss is preparing his own competition. So, when you get up early Monday morning, put a smile on your dial and realise what's really going on. Your boss is paying you for something I would pay him for! To train me to be his opposition! Competitor!! Or call it a job if it gets you a salary at the top.

The Trap of Trading Time for Money

Time is life's most limited commodity. Money, on the other hand, depreciates; it loses value every year. The tragedy? Most people trade their limited, precious time for money, then trade that money for liabilities that also lose value. It's a double loss instead, trade time for knowledge and experience. A job isn't just a wage; it's a paid apprenticeship in skills that can buy you freedom.

Tax Write-Offs the Smart Way

Too many business owners fall for the accountant's trick: "Buy a car, it's tax-deductible." Sure, but you're still bleeding cash on a liability for tax relief. I'd rather buy an asset (with a tax write-off as well) and turn it into an asset. A new BMW = $3,000 per month in repayments. -or-

Buy two or three Toyota Camrys for the same value and then rent them to Uber drivers for $2,400-$3600 per month in passive income. That's a $5,400- $6600 swing every single month.

Kayaks vs. Cars

My mate Chad (remember him from Big Brother?) is the perfect case study. He could've followed the standard accountant advice and bought a car for a quick tax write-off. Instead, he owns a gym/fitness business, so he bought 12 kayaks for $25,000 (tax write-off), registered a side business, and turned them into a daily rental operation. Now, those kayaks paddle past my house on Sydney Harbour daily. What was a tax write-off became a whole new income stream. Now, the kicker is that if he is fully booked 7 days a week, he could pay for his business in a week. That's unheard of. Remember the example I gave: you get an idea, another person might give you another, and then something can happen. This is a classic example. Chad had the idea bouncing around, and now it's a reality. With the help of a couple of friends and a mentor!

Iron sharpens iron. That's the power of creative thinking: "How can I turn this expense into an asset?"

Be Creative with Problems (The Covid Story)

During the lockdown, Chad and I were stopped by the police. Travel limit: 8 km. Chad passed all his questions. But then they picked on poor me.

We were going to his house over the bridge, it was only a 7-8 km drive, roughly, but only 1 km by air. The only exception to the rule: Visiting your partner! Quick thinking: "I pointed at Chad- I'm going to my partner's house, - "sorry sir "-

The police waved us through. (Now you can't blame Chad, I did the talking, he did the sweating). Hey! I can identify as anything I want to - even if he didn't! Lesson - Sometimes rules, like problems, require creativity. You can cry, "I can't," or you can find a path through. Chad wasn't my partner, except for that ride home.

Key Principle: Don't chase "looking rich." Build assets that make you rich. Don't trade time for wages. Trade it for knowledge and leverage. And when you hit a wall, get creative.

Appointments or Disappointments

We all have appointments in life. But if we don't show up to them, if we don't step into the moment, all we're left with is disappointment. Life throws plenty of those our way: lost jobs, breakups, and bills that never seem to stop coming. Sometimes it feels like we work ourselves into the ground just to survive the month. I'll never forget the day I decided survival wasn't enough. I was about 19 or 20 years old, working for a contractor at Monier Tiles. My job? Straightening aluminium moulds for clay roof tiles. All day, every day. Bang it on the table, file the grooves, repeat. On my feet, mind-numbed. One afternoon, I walked outside, looked up at the sky, and said to myself: "I cannot do this until I'm 65. I just can't." That was the day everything changed. I didn't have money. I didn't have a road map. But I had a new kind of fuel: vision. I started learning about money and real estate, and I gave myself something I hadn't had before, hope. Not a fairy tale, but a genuine belief that something better was ahead.

From Moulds to Marketing

Fast forward to today. I'm on a flight from Hamilton Island back to Sydney, tired but buzzing. I've been with my extended family, but my mind keeps turning over with my businesses, especially my newest one: laboratory-grown diamonds.

The biggest challenge? Awareness. People are not familiar enough with the product. And the truth is, you can be the best in the world at what you do, but if no one knows about you, it doesn't matter. If I started a lawn mowing business and even offered to mow for free tomorrow, it wouldn't matter unless I told people. Marketing isn't a luxury; it's oxygen for a business. I've always been passionate about learning about marketing. These days, there's Facebook, Instagram, TikTok, and all the usual social media apps that use keywords and target an audience. I will use those, but I'm also thinking bigger. What if I gave away an $11,000 engagement ring on the radio every month? My cost is only $2,500 to $5,000. That's a calculated bet: trade a diamond for massive exposure. Imagine the hook: Propose live on air, if she says yes, you win the ring. That's not just marketing. That's a story people remember.

Principle: Creativity Beats Cash

Both these stories remind me: business isn't just about money, it's about creativity. Anyone can play checkers. Few can play chess. You don't always need millions to market your product. Sometimes you just need one great idea, one clever angle, one bold move. The line between genius and crazy is thin, but if you're not crossing it occasionally, you're probably being too safe.

The Naughty Sons

My two sons are good, decent, law-abiding young men. They've never been in trouble with the law. But let me tell you, they are very naughty. Not bad. Just cheeky, clever, hilarious, and at times, downright dangerous to be around if you like keeping a straight face. One night, they attended a church conference in Sydney, where they were supposedly inspired and encouraged. Somewhere along the way, they found bright orange overalls belonging to council workers. And what do two smart, cheeky boys do with that? They went down to one of Australia's busiest roads, Parramatta Road, gathered up orange and black striped road barriers, and closed it. Completely. They detoured traffic into tiny side streets until chaos backed up everywhere. Rangers turned up furious, but even they couldn't help laughing.

Then there was our annual Father's Day ski trip, the three boys. My younger son found a walking cane belonging to a blind man. Add sunglasses, and suddenly we had "the blind skier." At the packed pub that night, the food and drink line was twenty minutes long, five people deep. My son picked up his cane, tapped his way through the crowd, and went straight to the front. Not one person stopped him. The waiter even offered to carry his drinks and food back to the table. If that wasn't enough, on his way back, he walked straight up to two loud, drunk American blokes, put the cane between their legs, and fell to the floor groaning in pain. They nearly fainted with guilt, apologising and helping him back to our table while I laughed so hard I could hardly breathe.

And of course, they saved their best prank for me. That same trip, I wasn't feeling well. My son offered me some antibiotics. I took two. Before bed, he asked if I wanted another. Sure, why not? In the morning, I wasn't much better, so I took one more. That's when they collapsed on the floor laughing. "Dad, those weren't antibiotics... they were laxatives." Let's just say skiing that day involved several unscheduled pit stops to the men's bathroom. They had no sympathy at all, but by the end of it, I'll admit I felt lighter, cleaner, and much better.

That's my boys. You are never safe when they are around. Naughty? Absolutely. Funny? Always. And they remind me of this truth:

"It's your life. Everyone else is just visiting. So, make sure you have fun and enjoy it as much as possible."

I remember talking to my ex-sister-in-law once, "I need to start speaking properly (less slang like 'yous' and 'youst to) '" She looked at me, innocent as ever, and replied: "You mean speak proper?" I couldn't help but laugh. She wasn't being cheeky, unlike my family. Let's just say this - she is socially a bit challenged and needs to act more proper.

Here's the thing: I don't want to come across as fake. I hate smiling for photos because it feels corny and forced. I want to grow, improve, and sharpen myself, but never lose my humour, my cheekiness, or my true self because nobody wants to be like a Bali Rolex, not even a genuine fake. One of the fake things we do as people is refuse to accept compliments. Think about it: we spend hours picking out a shirt. Try on thirty of them. Reject the ones that make us look fat, weird, or nerdy. Finally, we pick the one that makes us look good. Then someone comes along a week later and says, "Nice shirt, mate," and what do we do? We downplay it. "No, got it cheap at the shops." Why? Why can't we just say, "Thanks, I appreciate it"?

Imagine someone comes up to my partner and says, "Your man's very handsome." Now, imagine if she replied: "Nah, he's ten years older than me, got some grey hairs, no six-pack, I found him sitting alone at the discount rack." Funny, maybe true, but ridiculous! Yet that's exactly how we sound when we brush off a compliment. The truth is, a compliment costs nothing to give, but it carries real value. I go out of my way to offer one whenever I meet someone new. Shoes, watch, shirt, hair, something. Because people always remember the one who noticed. But not everyone takes it the right way.

My friend's boss, staring straight at me, once said to my face, in front of everyone at a bar, "I don't trust people who are always nice to me." I replied calmly, "Well, not everyone speaks nicely about you. In fact, I've already heard a few people tonight call you a dickhead." Then I smiled and turned slightly, continuing another conversation as though nothing had happened. He wasn't getting any more oxygen. Now, was that polite? Maybe not. But it was true. At times, people mistake kindness for weakness.

Where I grew up, you didn't argue with your mates; you gave them a right hook. But he had only ever seen me being polite and overly kind to everyone, so he assumed I was fake and a weak person.

He was shocked and not expecting me to respond the way I did, but in situations like this, I have to be mindful of my behaviour. I just won't tolerate it because I'm very deliberate about not causing upset or giving reason to behave that way towards me. I know I have a personality inside me that I put to bed and let sleep many years ago, and I don't desire to return to that person, but I think it is about self-respect and protection. I do it even with my father and my mother's husband. I love them, but they cannot take up a post they abandoned many years ago. And I will let them know if they do.

It reminds me of a man I supervised at the glass factory years ago. Nickname: Jabba, because he never shuts up. (For context, almost every guy has a nickname at work in Australia.) The best one is a guy - called 'Keth.' For years, everyone, even his bosses, thought his name was Keth. He had an eye -missing! And his actual name was Keith, but his workmates called him Keth.

Anyway, Jabba found out from someone that I used to be a bit of a wild kid, but I'd "changed" and was "churchy" now. He pipes up in the lunchroom, loud enough for everyone to hear: he looks at me, says, "So if I punch you in the face, will you turn the other cheek? "I smiled and said, Well, "I hope I would! But I tell you what, you'll be the first to find out - whether I turn the other cheek or put you in hospital. "The room erupted. Jabba went quiet. And I realised something: sometimes you've got to answer an idiot according to his folly. Not always, but sometimes.

I'm human. I mess up. I'm not always the example to follow. But people often mistake my kindness for weakness! -Don't be fake. - Accept compliments with humility. -And, sometimes you've got to let people know- they may not be stupid -but they act like idiots at times. - Kindness is strength, not weakness (sometimes I'm forced to remind people about this).

Unknown-Author

(((((((Dad Story No.1)

I've got a unique friendship with my dad. We're best mates. Out of the whole family, I'm the closest to him. I'm not saying I'm his favourite... I'm only hinting that I am :)) and just quietly, how could I not be. Now, I've got an ongoing thing with my dad: I prank him. But they've got to be good. Properly planned. And spaced out, minimum 1–2 years apart. Keeps him on his toes. Always new ideas. Always funny... Well, at least for me.

Years back, I was living in southwest Sydney. Dad was up in Cairns, the top part of Australia. I flew him down to stay with me and my family (three teenagers in the house, dangerous mix already). I'd prepared a special little surprise. I'd found an old lotto draw on YouTube. It was perfect, local news, a couple of TV ads, then the lotto numbers. Looked like the real deal. I wrote down the six numbers and kept them ready. Now, my lovely and terrible daughter (17 at the time) was in on it. When Pop arrived, she said sweetly, "Pop, I can't put lotto on, I'm underage. Can you put it on for me today?" Of course, he said yes.

Later that day, we stopped at a lotto shop. I quietly filled out a card with the six magic numbers (without him noticing) and added five auto-pick games. Handed it over and said, "Dad, can you pay for that while I grab the coffees?" He paid, had the real ticket in his hand. Stage one complete. 8 pm comes. Lotto time. My daughter asks, "Can we watch it, Pop?" I say, "No, I'm watching the footy. Put it on my iPad." Dad didn't know what an iPad was; he thought it was a little TV. So, we press play on the YouTube clip. The news comes on. Ads play. Looks legit. Then the draw starts. One by one, the numbers drop. My dad and daughter are circling them. First ball... match. Second ball... match. By the time the sixth one drops, Dad's up on his feet, pale, shaking, swearing like only he can: "Son... read those numbers out again." I did. He blurts out, "F... hell, we've won!!!" My daughter goes, "How much, Pop?"

"Six million dollars, darling. SIX MILLION." Then Dad, with the voice of Moses on the mountain, goes: "F... me! Six numbers, no supps!" We all go nuts. He's pacing the room, half crying, half in shock. Meanwhile, I've already lost it. Laughing too hard, tears streaming down my face. He stops. Narrows his eyes. "You're taking the piss, aren't ya?" I shake my head, still laughing. He asks again. I can't even answer. Finally, I nod yes.

Well, he starts kicking me! I'm on the floor crying with laughter, he's half crying too, shouting: "You bastard! You got me. You bloody got me." And he's right. I did.

But here's the thing, Dad now gets to tell people he knows what it feels like to win six million bucks... just not what it feels like to spend it. And he loves telling that story to anyone new we meet. Every time. And honestly? So do I. :))

Run in Your Own Lane

Often in life, we look at other people's wins and successes, and it's tempting to think: "If I just do what they did, I'll get what they got." It seems logical, doesn't it? Just copy their formula. Follow their blueprint. Emulate their steps.

But the truth is, their path isn't yours.

What worked for them was the product of their personality, timing, experiences, opportunities, and unique strengths. Copying someone else's strategy rarely leads to the same destination because you're not starting from the same place. At best, imitation will make you a second-rate version of someone else. At worst, it will make you frustrated, burnt out, and confused about why your results don't match theirs.

The Beat of Your Own Drum

I've always walked to a different beat. My drumbeat isn't the most popular one of the year, nor the one that makes the crowd move in sync. And honestly? That's the point. I've never wanted to be part of the crowd. I'd rather play my beat boldly and let the crowd decide whether to dance or not.

People say they like uniqueness. They applaud individuality. They post quotes about authenticity. But the truth is, uniqueness is often only celebrated when it fits inside the box people are comfortable with. The moment your rhythm challenges them, the applause quiets. Instead of being inspired, some people feel threatened. Instead of admiring your courage, they compare your difference to their sameness and label themselves as failures.

That's why you must guard your rhythm fiercely. Find your lane, own it, and run with conviction. Because if you don't, the world will always try to pull you back into conformity.

CHAPTER 13

THE COST OF COMPARISON

With your exact combination of talents, scars, gifts, and vision. That's not an accident. That's design.

Comparison is a thief. It robs you of joy, distorts your perspective, and convinces you that your lane isn't good enough. But here's the truth: your lane doesn't need to look like anyone else's because it's not supposed to.

If you waste your energy looking sideways, you'll miss what's ahead of you. No sprinter in a race wins by staring into the lane next to them. They run eyes forward, laser-focused on their own finish line. The same applies to life and business. Your energy must go into your race, not theirs.

Growth Through Letting Go

Here's something people don't always realise: growth is not always about adding more. Sometimes, it's about subtracting. Letting go. Releasing.

We often cling to things that once served us but now limit us:

A salary that keeps us comfortable but stops us from chasing our business dreams.

A role or title that gave us identity, but now feels like a cage. Habits that once helped us survive but now keep us stagnant.

Think of the blind man's cane. For a time, it is essential. It keeps him steady, helps him navigate, and protects him from harm. But if one day he regains his sight, what once was his lifeline can become his limitation. The cane is no longer necessary, and clinging to it does nothing but get in his way.

The same is true for us. What got you here may not get you there. Tools, relationships, and even mindsets that once carried you forward can become the very things that hold you back if you don't release them at the right time.

Your Unique Lane

Running in your own lane doesn't mean ignoring wisdom or refusing to learn from others. It means filtering advice through the lens of your unique design. It means asking: Does this align with who I am? Does this move me toward my race, not theirs?

Your lane is not about speed or comparison. It's about alignment. And when you run aligned, when your rhythm matches your purpose, progress feels natural, not forced.

Closing Reflection

There is freedom in realising you don't need to copy anyone else. You were not created to be their echo. You were designed to be a voice, a rhythm, a lane all your own.

So, stop clinging to the cane. Stop staring into the next lane. Plant your feet in yours. Run your race. Play your beat. And let the world adjust to your rhythm instead of the other way around.

The Blind Man at the Bus Stop

Speaking of blind men - this happened today.

I'd just dropped my son off at the train station in Sydney and was about to drive off when I spotted a guy walking towards the bus stop. White cane with the round tip, sunnies on, moving carefully. A blind man. I remember thinking, imagine navigating through all this chaos without sight: the traffic, the crowds, the noise. I actually felt for him. Life would be tough. Anyway, he tapped his way right up to the bus shelter and, dead set, landed exactly where the seat was. Perfect. He must've been familiar with the area. So far, so normal. Then he did something that threw me. He pulled up his sleeve, tilted his wrist, and looked down at his watch. Not a talking smartwatch. Not some fancy device. Just an old-school, little round-face watch. Now I'm sitting in the car gripping the wheel, biting my tongue so I don't burst out laughing. And then... he looked up. Not vaguely, not randomly, straight in my direction. With the tiniest grin. At that point, I lost it. I'm cracking up, can't even drive, tears running down my face. Now look, I don't want to mock the bloke. But honestly? He wasn't looking too blind at that moment! What was going on there? I've got no idea. Perhaps he had some insight, maybe it was a trick, possibly he just enjoyed messing with people. All I know is, I would love to know what game he was playing. Curiosity!!!

The Rule of 7

There's a fascinating principle in communication and influence called The Rule of 7. It's the idea that someone needs to hear a message around seven times before they'll believe it, remember it, or take action.

This concept dates back to advertising research from the 1930s to the 1950s, when marketers observed a clear pattern: repetition-built familiarity, and familiarity in turn-built trust. Back then, movie studios used the rule to promote new films. They learned that if people encountered the same title seven times on posters, radio spots, and billboards, they were far more likely to buy a ticket.

Decades later, the principle hasn't changed. If anything, it has become even more critical in today's noisy, information-saturated world.

Why Repetition Works

Familiarity

The human brain is wired to prefer what it recognises. Psychologists refer to this phenomenon as the mere exposure effect. The more often we see or hear something, the more familiar and trustworthy it feels. Even if the message hasn't fully sunk in, our brains relax around what's familiar.

Overcoming Doubt

The first time someone hears an idea, scepticism often kicks in: "That won't work for me." The second or third time, the resistance softens. By the fifth or sixth exposure, the idea begins to sound less like a suggestion and more like common sense.

Cutting Through Noise

People are bombarded with thousands of messages daily, emails, texts, ads, conversations, and headlines. Most vanish instantly. Repetition ensures your message doesn't just blend into the noise. It gives your words staying power.

Beyond Advertising

While the Rule of 7 originated in marketing, it applies to every area of life and leadership:

- In business, A leader who repeats core values and vision ensures the team doesn't just hear them once; they live them.
- In personal growth, affirmations, goals, or new habits require repeated reinforcement before they take hold.
- In relationships, Expressions of love, encouragement, or gratitude don't lose meaning with repetition; they gain it.

The Rule of 7 is really the rule of persistence. It reminds us that people don't usually change after hearing something once. Change happens when the message becomes a drumbeat, steady and undeniable.

CHAPTER 14

THE SHADOW SIDE OF REPETITION

Repetition is powerful, but it must be used with care. Too much, delivered poorly, becomes noise, nagging, or manipulation. The art is in repeating your message with variation, creativity, and sincerity so it feels consistent without becoming stale.

Empty slogans repeated without action lose impact.

A message repeated with genuine passion gains force with every echo.

Putting the Rule of 7 to Work

Here's how to use the principle wisely:

Say it in different ways. People learn through stories, visuals, facts, and emotions. Rotate your delivery so the same truth lands on various levels.

Integrate it everywhere. If you're a leader, weave your core message into meetings, emails, recognition moments, and decisions. When building a brand, ensure your values are consistently reflected across all platforms.

Anchor with action. Repetition only sticks if it's reinforced by behaviour. Words alone fade; words plus action become unshakeable.

Stay patient. Don't assume lack of response means failure. Often, you're just on repetition number three, and the breakthrough is still coming.

Closing Reflection

The Rule of 7 isn't just about marketing; it's about influence, leadership, and legacy. Messages that matter need repetition. Truth needs repeating. Vision needs reminding. Love needs reaffirming.

So don't grow weary of saying the same thing seven or seventy times. Because the seventh time you speak may be the first time someone truly listens.

Today's Adaptation

With social media and the constant flow of information, some say it might take 15–20 touches instead of just 7. (Guys - you might get a slap if you push past 7! - Just a warning. However, the principle remains the same: consistency and repetition foster belief and influence.

I'm a big believer in this type of thinking - I make sure to tell my partner how beautiful she is and how much I love her. I know that when I'm told something similar, I don't dislike it. - I may repeat sayings and thoughts in this book; I want it to sink in. If you can read this book and have three or more memorable things that you can repeat for the rest of your life, I'd say I've done my job!

Words of Encouragement

Everyone needs encouragement. Everyone. And the best part? It costs nothing to be nice. So, let me ask you, how often do you get encouraged? And when was the last time you encouraged someone else? I personally believe encouragement is one of the most powerful things we can give. When I meet someone new, I make it a point to compliment something about them, but only if it's genuine. No fake fluff. I wouldn't say to a bloke who clearly smashes -Macca's five nights a week, "Gee mate, you look fantastic." That isn't very respectful. But I could look him in the eye and say, "Love your jacket, mate, where did you pick that up? Looks sharp." It's incredible how far a genuine word goes!

Encouraging Mates

Some of the closest friendships I've built with younger men started simply because I encouraged them. I'd call them a legend, a champion, sometimes serious, sometimes joking. But I meant it. One of my closest mates told me straight up: "I've never had another man- not family, not friends, ever tell me they were proud of me or that they loved me until I meet you." That hit me. Hard. We forget that men need it too. In fact, guys probably get encouraged a lot less than women do. That's why I make a point to say it. To my mates. To my family. To my sons. To men who've maybe never once heard it in their life: "I'm proud of you, mate." or "I appreciate you."

Encouraging Women

Of course, women need encouragement just as much. I dated a woman once who, in my eyes, was stunning. I'd often tell her she looked beautiful. One night, I asked why she never really believed me, and she said, "Because I know I'm okay, but I'm not beautiful. My ex of 15 years never once told me I was beautiful." That floored me. Imagine being with someone for 15 years and never once hearing that? Now, was she a 10-out-of-10 supermodel? No. But to me, she was beautiful. And if you find someone beautiful, you should tell them. It's simple, be genuine and Real- Men and Women, Everyone. We all need compliments, encouragement, and someone to believe in us. We need to be told we're doing okay, that we matter, that we're appreciated. So, if you're reading this

Here's your reminder: don't hold back. Encourage someone. Compliment someone. Tell them you're proud of them. Don't tell your workmate - beautiful … you don't want HR knocking on your door. - Unless it is the HR lady, and you want her knocking on your door. :)

Saying Sorry & Forgiveness

Saying sorry isn't about getting forgiveness. It's about admitting you're wrong and letting the person know you regret what you did. Forgiveness is not automatic; it's a gift. When you apologise, you're accepting fault. Whether or not the other person forgives you, that's on them. Forgiveness is for the offended; it releases their hurt, it heals them. But too often we treat "sorry" like a legal right: "I said sorry, so you must accept it, shake my hand, and move on." Life doesn't work like that. If you apologise and the other person doesn't forgive you, you've still done what's right. Don't say sorry so that you can feel justified. Do it because you mean it. Be kind-hearted.

It'll open doors you couldn't ever open yourself. And hey, next time someone says sorry to you, or you need to say sorry to someone else, remember: it takes courage and humility. Just saying.

"Just Follow Your Heart"

I'm not a fan of people saying, "Just follow your heart." Now, I know I mentioned earlier the importance of "guarding your heart." That's about protecting what's important and combining Logic and reasoning. This is different. This "follow your heart" business is usually code for following your feelings. Which, let's be honest, are impulsive, irrational, and half the time full of nonsense. Don't get me wrong, I'm all for pursuing your dreams and passions. But the advice to "just follow your heart" often really means: it's okay to quit, it's OK to break promises, it's OK to give up if it feels good. That's not selfless. That's selfish. I know this might rub people the wrong way, but hey, I'm sorry. You've got to forgive me, remember! Joking... And yes, you won't agree with everything I say, but you're entitled to be wrong occasionally. :)

I told a partner that I was wrong once. She smiled and said, "What was it?" I said, "That I thought I was wrong. I was actually right, but wrong in thinking I was wrong." Even she laughed.

The Problem with "Just Follow Your Heart"

Our hearts are deceitful a lot of the time. Think of your first big love. For most of us, it was a fantastic experience. But 10–20 years later? Most aren't still with that first love. In fact, some can no longer stand the person. How can we feel so deeply one decade, and nothing the next? People who last 20, 30, 40 years together don't "follow their heart." Because if they did, they'd have left after five. Lasting relationships are built on choices. On forgiveness. On letting go- deciding to love when the heart doesn't feel like it. That's why we must guard our hearts.

Don't let bitterness or anger take root. Don't let a hurt heart drive your choices, because broken hearts have destroyed marriages, families, and businesses.

There's an old proverb: the heart is deceitful and tells lies. People who live by the phrase "just follow your heart" are usually not emotionally mature. It's a dangerous way to live. Sure, sometimes we follow what our heart wants, but it should never be the compass for the most significant decisions in life when our hearts are not healthy and actually broken.

Learning Through Mistakes

So, what about when we make a mistake? For me, I decided years ago that every challenging situation I went through, even those that looked terrible at the start, I'd learn from it. I'd grow. I'd become wiser, more compassionate, bigger-hearted. When I went through my jail experience, I learnt two huge things- first, what actually mattered: family and close friends. Second, not everyone in trouble got there through stupidity or bad behaviour. Sometimes life traps you.

But even then, you can grow. I came out more empathetic, less judgmental. When I got divorced (not my choice), I felt like a failure. Embarrassed. I thought I'd let my family down. But that season shaped me, too. I realised relationships aren't easy, and not everyone is suited for each other. Still, I believe we should fight for our marriages before giving up. I also saw where I fell short. I probably took my ex-wife for granted, and didn't help enough at home. I justified it with "I work two jobs and run a business, I'm tired." But looking back, I see the weight she carried, too. Now? I'm different. When I have a partner, I like the house to be tidy, a meal ready, maybe even a candle on the table. And when we're not dining in, I love going to nice restaurants, rooftops, and waterfront spots. Because I learnt. And I changed.

Another Aussie (a friend of my mate Matt) started a T-shirt label called Attitude. He couldn't break into surf shops, so he hacked human psychology. He'd get people to call stores and ask for Attitude shirts, act disappointed when told "no," and even show up pretending to be customers desperate for them. Then, a few days later, he'd walk in as a rep, offering to stock the "famous" brand everyone was asking for. It worked. The shirts sold. And a few years later? He sold the brand to Panasonic for a considerable sum.

Business Lessons from the Hard Yards

I've started a few businesses that either cost me too much money, too much time, or, in some cases, actually lost me money. But here's the thing: I learnt so much from each one. Every mistake gave me an education you can't buy, and that's what helped me build or buy better ones later. Life's a learning experience, even the painful bits. Even when working for someone else, I never just saw it as "a job." I saw it as the boss paying me to learn skills, to build contacts, and to prepare myself, maybe one day to become his competition.

Don't see your job as some tedious 9–5 chore. See it as training. See it as networking. See it as preparing the future YOU. Now, I'm not pretending I thought like this all my life. I didn't. But as I've grown older, I can see the value in it, and that's what I pass on to my younger mates. Work hard. Be the best employee. First to arrive, last to leave. Before you leave, ask your boss if there's anything they need you to do before you go. Little things like that can speed up your career more than you think.

Take one of my younger brothers, for example. He was selling flooring, soft rubber for playgrounds and schools. I said to him, 'Get contacts.' Help your customers and suppliers exceed their expectations. If you do that, they'll stay loyal. Find gaps. Offer your boss something new, like a product he doesn't stock, maybe ceramic tiles, either cut him in on the deal or run it as a side hustle after hours. See, suppliers are readily available. Buyers are the gold. Anybody can source a product, but not everybody can sell it. That's what I tried to teach my brother: his value was in knowing buyers and companies already. Why not use that? And don't forget, his boss was paying him every week to learn the trade, to meet suppliers, to get to know the buyers, to learn quoting, delivery, relationship building, all the headaches a business deals with.

If I wanted to start a flooring business from scratch, I'd pay his boss to train me for six months. Think about it - he was literally being paid to learn. Now let's talk stats. Please don't quote me exact numbers, but it's roughly like this: When a business starts, it has a roughly 20% chance of surviving for five years. After 10 years, only about 20% of the 20% survivors are still around after 10 years, and 60% of those survivors are franchises. That means having your own business for 10 years is rare, which is why banks are hesitant to lend to start-ups.

That's why most CEOs end up signing personal guarantees; if the business folds, they're personally on the hook. So, here's my point: when you start, you want the best foundation possible. Learn from mistakes (yours or others'), build contacts, and position yourself to be in that small percentage that actually makes it long-term. I honestly feel that for people who start with enthusiasm and energy, it's often clear where it'll end. Not because they're bad people, but because they didn't have the plan, the homework, or the industry experience. Sure, there are brilliant exceptions, Facebook, Spotify, Instagram, but for every one of those, there are thousands that failed. I hope this helps you think differently about work, business, and building your future. Nothing happens without hard work and planning, but if you do the prep right, you'll set yourself apart.

The real skill is getting buyers. Don't waste your 9–5. Use it as your training ground for your 5–9.

Don't compare, run in your own lane.

Why is it that some people seem to do well in everything they touch, while others feel like they're constantly struggling just to get ahead? I think there are many reasons, but I also don't think it's healthy to compare ourselves to others. At my age, with my background, I've done reasonably well. However, I've friends both older and younger who are financially ahead of me. Some of them are much more "successful" by the world's standards. But here's the truth, I haven't lived their life. I didn't have their education, their opportunities, or their setbacks. And they didn't have mine. Everyone is running their own race.

Take, for example, one of my younger brothers. He's highly educated, a professor in psychology, and has travelled the world. Yet, financially, he has little in the way of assets and earns less than most of my other brothers. But has he failed? Absolutely not. He's the only one of us who completed university, and he's carved out a great career. He values education and travel above money. Me? I value time and assets. Different goals. Different lanes. That's why jealousy and envy are such small-minded ways to think.

When I see someone succeed, I don't think, "He's showing off" or "she doesn't deserve it." I think, "If they can do it, why can't I?" I celebrate people's wins. I send big congratulations when someone gets promoted, starts a business, or buys a house—last night I found out my young friend Kyara, who was working for Deloitte, just moved to Macquarie Bank on a 40% pay rise. She's only 24. I was pumped for her! I told her we'd celebrate her new job and my birthday together. Why not get excited for the people around you? It feels so much better than being jealous.

However, the sad truth is that sometimes people can become jealous. Instead of being inspired, it highlights their own lack of success or their failures. Again, that's because they're comparing. Kyara had strong parents in corporate jobs, good family support, and the chance to live at home, study, save, and build her career. That wasn't my path. But I don't see my life as a failure compared to hers. She worked hard, played smart, went to social events, built friendships at work, and made herself valuable. That's why she's doing well. Here's the key: I never "network." I build relationships. Networks are shallow. Relationships are the key.

Let me give you an example. I own a mattress business that sells through physiotherapists and chiropractors. My supplier, Allen, is a Chinese guy in Sydney. Initially, he was my supplier, and I was his customer. But I started hanging out with him, visited his factories in China and Sydney, and even began learning Mandarin.

He asked me to accompany him to trade shows in China and play the role of a "raving customer." We turned it into holidays and fun trips together. Now he's not just a supplier, he's my gèrmén -meaning best mate, like a brother, in Mandarin. We're close mates. I no longer bother asking him for prices. I know he'll look after me. And I want him to make money too. It goes both ways. That's what happens when you build relationships instead of just networks. He cares about my business, and I care about his. That's priceless. We've had so many great holidays and nights out together, and one day, I'd love to do something bigger with him in China. Who knows where that relationship will go? Don't compare your chapter 5 to someone else's chapter 20.

Networking builds contacts. Relationships Build Loyalty - Celebrate Others' Wins. If you can't be happy for someone else, you'll never be truly happy for yourself.

Discipline = Real Freedom

Being disciplined isn't about restriction; it's about freedom. Absolute freedom is self-control. The undisciplined are slaves to every little whim, trend, and shiny distraction that comes along. I find it hilarious when people say, "Oh, you're missing out," just because someone chooses to get fitter, wealthier, or happier, and then claim they're missing out. That's not freedom. That's just being a sheep, doing what everyone else does -broke, unhealthy, unhappy. They blow their money on weekends, come home depressed, and then do it all over again. I see it all the time. Men at nice bars, splashing cash to look successful. Then you talk to them, and they brag about their "big job" or their "business that's killing it." But Monday morning, they're back at work, chained to the grind—weekend millionaires.

True success is choice. If you're genuinely successful, you don't have to get up and go to work Monday morning, unless you actually love what you do. Personally, I'd rather sleep in and wander down to my favourite cafe by the beach. That's freedom.

Stop Explaining Yourself

Another thing I've learnt, I don't owe everyone an explanation. Some people ask out of curiosity, seeking to debate, argue, or cross-examine your choices. I don't play that game anymore. If someone's pushing, I'll simply smile, shrug, or ask them questions back: "What do you mean? Why are you asking?" Nine times out of ten, they tie themselves in knots. Sometimes the best response is no response at all. If someone is genuinely interested in learning, by all means, ask away. I'll never forget what an old mentor told me: "Don't give oxygen to stupid conversations." He said, "Most people like that are just trying to start fires. And fires can't grow without oxygen." That line stuck with me for life, and it's saved me from wasting hours in pointless arguments.

Difficult People & Arguments

Let's be honest, difficult people are part of life. You can't avoid them all, but you don't have to let them drain you. Some deals or contracts simply aren't worth the headache. I'd rather walk away and keep the peace, avoiding the argument. These days, I see them differently. Suppose I'm genuinely helping someone see a better way, fair enough. But if I'm only arguing to prove I'm more intelligent, sharper, or more articulate, that's not wisdom. That's just my ego chasing a win. Winning an argument but losing peace is a dumb victory. Discipline isn't a cage; it leads to freedom. Weekend millionaires will always be weekend millionaires. Don't fuel dumb fires, starve them of oxygen. Argue to help, not to win. Peace is more valuable than proving you're right.

Saturday night at 7:30 p.m., I received a phone call. To my surprise, it was my doctor. Now, we're not mates, but I had just had my prostate checked and blood tests done. He said that after reviewing my results, I needed to come in first thing Monday morning for an MRI because things "don't look good." (Which, let's be real, usually means the big "C".) So, I asked him straight: "Mate, what's the deal? Just be upfront with me." He repeated himself: "I'm not 100% sure yet, but things don't look great. Let's wait until Monday to talk."

Not the kind of phone call you expect on a Saturday night. And here's the kicker, at the moment, my stepmother has cancer and probably won't see out the year, and recently, my father as well, and now I'm being thrown into this unknown. It doesn't exactly sound good when your doctor calls after hours instead of waiting until Monday morning. Still, I'm glad he called. At least we can get on top of it quickly. It's a strange feeling. I'm not scared for myself. I don't feel panicked or worried. But I am sad for my partner and my three amazing kids (all adults now).

I hate the thought of them watching me go through this, then possibly losing me altogether. As for me, I don't fear death. I'm confident I'll end up next to my mum in glory, listening to her long, boring stories again. (Can't wait for that part). So, it's up in the air. I'm not negative, and I'm not a drama queen. I'm practical, I'm logical. However, I'm also holding onto the hope that things will work out. Life will be ok.

We'll see. I'll let you know how it goes. And hey, if you get about 70% through this book and it suddenly ends, then I guess you know why. :) joking.

Friendships / Partners / Business Connections

Getting the right circle, the people you do life with, is everything. Your tight group, your partner, your business partner... these are the ones who shape you more than anyone else.

Sometimes suffering is the only way we realise certain people shouldn't have been in our lives as long as they were. We often hold on out of habit, loyalty, or just being "too nice," but the truth is, not everyone deserves a long-term seat at our table. One of the hardest lessons I learned was assuming people think the same way I do. Most don't. That's not right or wrong, it's just reality. But when you expect others to act how you would, disappointment is almost guaranteed. Friendships break. Partnerships crack. And business relationships collapse. The key is accepting people for who they are instead of wasting energy trying to change them. That's freedom, the

96

freedom to live your life, to do what feels right, without being chained to the approval of people who, let's be honest, often won't even be around in three to five years. With partners, I had to learn this the hard way: you can't make someone love you more by doing more of what they already don't appreciate. If someone loves you, they just do. Love doesn't grow from persuasion; it grows from presence. That's who we should all be chasing, not the person who constantly makes you feel like you're not enough, or like you've got to earn their love with more money, more looks, or more effort. That's not love. That's selfish and sad.

I'll never forget being in China on a business trip. This lady, totally straight-talking (as the Chinese often are), said to me: "If you weren't so fat, you'd be handsome." So, I replied, "If you were beautiful, you could be a model." Both were true. I was overweight back then (I've since lost it, so maybe I am handsome now), and she definitely wasn't model material. To be fair, she wasn't ugly, just more of a "6," but thought she was a "9." I don't try to change people to date or befriend. Either they're right for me, or they're right for someone else. And to be fair to her, she wasn't trying to be mean, just blunt.

But here's the thing: growth and change should come from you, not from someone else's demands. Over the last decade, I've changed my weight, eating habits, style, and even the way I treat people. Not because a girl asked me to, but because I wanted to. Because I admired how certain men carried themselves, I tried to emulate them and improve myself. Sure, when you're with a partner, you do make minor adjustments. If you love them, you don't want to keep doing things that upset or offend them. But at the same time, you've got to stay true to yourself.

Early on in dating, my humour was too much for her. I had to tone it down a little. (Not much, though.) For example, we were flying to Cairns once, and I suggested she join the Jetstar membership club to save money on flights. I asked her three times, but she didn't do it. Then, when the hostess walked by, I whispered, "Quick, ask if you can join the Mile High Club." So, in her gorgeous Brazilian accent, she stopped the hostess and said, "Excuse me, can I join the Mile High Club?" The lady stopped, looked shocked, then smiled and asked, "Did your partner tell you to ask that?" My partner said yes, and the hostess just walked off grinning. My partner had no idea what it meant, and when I explained it later, she wasn't as amused as I was. But later, the hostess came back and told us the whole crew had cracked up when they heard the story. So, I said: "See, it was funny!" She disagreed, but we've found our balance. I've toned down 6%, and she's come up 60%. We're getting there.

Something I was taught years ago has stuck with me: The first to apologise is the bravest. The first to forgive is the strongest. The first to forget is the happiest. People often mistake my kindness for weakness. But here's the truth: not everyone we meet is meant to be in our lives forever. Some are here for a season, some to teach us what love feels like, some to teach us what pain feels like. That's life. I like to think my front door is always open and welcoming, but my back door is never locked either. People are free to come in, and just as free to leave.

The same goes for business partners and investors. Don't force someone into your circle just because they have money, skills, or influence. If the values don't align, the cracks will show, and when they do, it can cost you more than just money. The right business partner is like the right friend or partner: they make the journey lighter, not heavier. They add fuel to the fire, not smoke. And when you build with the right people, you don't just make money, you create something that lasts.

Thinking

If you've read a few chapters by now, you'll see a pattern. I keep circling back to thinking. Attitudes. Mindsets. The way we speak to ourselves. Why? Because every successful person, every mental health professional, every old person with real wisdom will tell you the same thing: your thinking is everything. "As a man thinks in his heart, so he will be."

When I was younger, if I stuffed up or said something dumb, I'd mutter to myself: "You idiot. Why did you do that? You're so stupid." I think many people do the same. But years ago, I changed that. These days, I'd never call myself stupid, and I'd never call someone else stupid either. Instead, I might say: "Don't act stupid because you're not." Or I'll tell myself: "Come on, mate, you're better than that.

Be patient, time is your friend. The solution is around the corner." How we talk to ourselves often spills over into how we speak to others. And it matters. Words cut deeper than we think. I'll give you an example. My eldest son, one of my best friends (I have about four best friends, okay), was going through a rough patch. He'd had a breakup, was travelling interstate, heartbroken, stressed, impatient, snappy. One day, we disagreed on something (I was, of course, right), and he called me an idiot. I pulled him up straight away: "Listen, son. Firstly, don't speak to me like that. I'm your dad. Secondly, I'm your boss." He apologised quickly. I knew it was just the season he was in, but still, I won't accept that, and nor should anyone. Unless, of course, they're actually an idiot (just joking).

"It's not I can't — but how can I"

This one sentence has shaped my entire life. It's how I built self-storage units. How I bought properties that have cash flow like clockwork. How I landed contracts worth millions. I remember my first big contract; I thought it'd be worth half a million. It turns out to be more like $9–11 million. I freaked out at first, "How the heck am I going to get 30 extra staff, cover 60 days of wages, and buy all the equipment?" But I held onto that thought: "It's not I can't, but how can I?" And it worked out. One of my suppliers, a Christian bloke who sponsors kids through his business, gave me 90 days' credit on everything I needed. He didn't even ask for the money.

I secured financing for some gear, bought a few older vehicles with cash, and completed a trade-in deal on another machine. I used some of my own money to cover wages, but then the client paid in 30 days anyway. Problem solved. Contract secured. And that mindset has carried me through every challenge since. Sometimes you just need faith. Believe it'll work out. And push until it does.

Leadership & Respect

When I interact with staff, I always strive to speak in the way I'd want a boss to talk to me - Respect first. Calmness always. But now and then, you've got to be tough. Once, one of our employees stood over a lady in our team and abused her. I couldn't let that slide. I walked straight over, stood in front of him, and said: "If you ever speak to one of (my) team like that again, I'll drag you out by your shirt and send you on your way." I made sure I said my! Meaning - being rude to (my) - involves me. Maybe I said a few other choice words, too. Can't quite remember. Another time, my head supervisor started letting power get to his head. He kept saying "my team" and "my workers" and threatening to sack people. One day, in front of the staff, he even told me to "F... off" on the phone-loudspeaker. So, I called him into the office in front of the whole team. I said:

"First, let's deal with you telling me to F... off. If you want to talk like that, we can go outside and deal with it man to man, and I won't be talking either." He went very quiet. He grew up in my neighbourhood and knew me when I was a teenager. Then I said, "Second, you don't have a team. You don't pay wages. Until you do, stop saying 'my workers.' I don't even call them that, and I own the company. They're not my staff, they're our team. These people give their time and effort to us. Show some respect." Respect isn't about being the boss.

It's about treating people as humans, whether in the office or outside. That's always been my style. If I bump into my staff outside of work, I introduce them as 'we work together. 'I don't even use the term 'we are equal'- we are not. If I say I'm equal to you, I am assuming I'm just as good, polite, kind, mature, and patient; I know I'm not. I might even be better at one of them than you, but maybe: maybe one. I should esteem and respect others. Demanding equality is screaming, 'I'm insecure.' Also, I love my daughter. But we are not equal. Not even close. She is way better than everyone :)).

CHAPTER 15

THE SHIFT

After a run-in with my mother's husband again, and this time, I put him in a position where he sat down quietly. (The whole story is later in the book) That moment changed everything. He knew then what I knew; he didn't hold authority in my life. He had never tried to be a stepdad, and he didn't get that privilege. From that day on, something shifted. Even now, at family events, he'll pull up my brothers if they cross a line, but never me. He knows he doesn't have that place. We are great now, no problem at all. But he knows! Instead, I became like a dad to my brothers, including my older brother. I taught him how to shave and manage his money, but I always showed him respect. He knew I was the big brother. I guided, protected, and helped them because nobody else did. My mum's husband missed that chance. My dad did too. They stepped away, and I stepped in.

I had to pull my dad up once, only a few years back - my younger brother flew into Sydney, single and young. I said, 'Get a train, and I will pick you up from the station.' Well, my dad found out and had a go at me in front of my brother. I told my dad -firmly: "Hey, Dad, I love you, but you left us here in Sydney and we

three boys are tight. We have our own family thing at times that doesn't involve you. (I knew it would cut him) -When we three argue, you stay out of it, because you will always lose and never come between us boys. You lost that years ago, sorry. I like to think I am kind-hearted and easy-going.

However, when boundaries are crossed and they move beyond their place of authority, I will call it out. I'm loyal; I won't leave a brother stranded. However, if you leave me stranded, I will forgive you, but I will never rely on you or let you think you can either. I'm a father, brother, best mate till the day I die - until you choose for me not to be. I've never allowed my family, marriage, relationships, or friendships with my brothers and sister to feel disbanded - not even a friend. It just isn't in my DNA. That's leadership - leaders don't bail.

Who Holds the Place

Here's the truth I've learned: authority belongs to the one who steps up and takes responsibility. My mum's husband and my dad both lost that place because they walked away. I didn't.

And I've carried that lesson into other parts of life. Authority isn't about a title. It isn't about demanding respect. It's about showing up, taking responsibility, and earning it. And you can't expect to get what you're not willing to give. Even in relationships, if I leave my post. That place isn't mine anymore. Authority only belongs where you've earned it. If you don't step into your place, someone else will. Families, businesses, and relationships are all the same. Responsibility creates authority, and authority creates respect. Lose one, and you lose them all. And don't expect it back in a hurry.

Wisdom, Advice & Humility

Here's another thing about thinking: how do you take advice? Some people love it. They grow fast. They stay teachable. However, many men (usually between 20 years old to 60, give or take 20 years) struggle to handle it. They don't like being told anything, especially if they're in business or high up in management. Pride gets in the way. Proverbs says: "A wise man increases in learning and takes instruction." I once heard an old guy say, "You've got two ears and one mouth. Use them accordingly." Fair call. Real wisdom doesn't just come with age. It comes from humility- listening, learning, staying teachable. That's why I keep people in my life who can speak into mine. One for business and finance, another for relationships, life, and even spiritual things. Sometimes they'll tell me my jokes aren't funny (not true). Sometimes they'll stop me from making a dumb decision. And usually, they're right, though don't tell them I said that. The truth is, we all need people who can keep us accountable, even kick us in the butt when needed. Without that, too many of us plateau.

Catch your "self-talk". Next time you say something negative about yourself, "I'm dumb," "I can't," "I always fail," stop and re-frame it. Replace it with: "I'm learning." Or "I can figure this out." Or "How can I?" Do this once a day for a month, and you'll be stunned at how much it rewires your thinking. Because here's the truth: what you say to yourself today is shaping the person you'll be tomorrow.

"No"- how do you deal with No as an answer

Is it permanent or not yet? How do you feel when someone says no? A flat-out no. The truth is, sometimes no is only for now. It's not always final. A parent saying no, a boss saying no to a pay rise, or a bank saying no to a loan, most of the time, those answers are based on circumstances: emotions, timing, finances, or just where someone's head is at in that moment. Take my daughter, for example. She was about 14 or 15 at the time, and like many teenagers, she had turned into a walking encyclopedia, debating her mother on everything. They were butting heads every day.

Then she wanted to go to a school dance, but her mother's answer was an immediate no. So, I sat my daughter down and said, "When the time is right, go sit on Mum's lap and say, 'Mum, I've noticed recently we're not getting along so well, but I want you to know I love you and you're my best friend.'" (Which was true.) I also told her to start helping out around the house without being asked. After a few days of hugs and kindness, she tried again: "Mum, I know you said no to the dance, and I'll respect that if it's final, but if you change your mind, just let me know." Let's just say by Friday night, she was in the most stunning dress, dancing the night away.

It's the same with work. Asking for a pay rise is not about barging into your boss's office and demanding more money. Timing is everything. Wait until the company is doing well, when sales are up, and new contracts have been secured. Make sure you've had some personal wins too- closed deals, put in extra effort, maybe worked the weekend.

Then sit down and start with something like: "I've really enjoyed working here lately. I feel like I'm getting so much more done in this environment. And in saying that, I don't want to put you on the spot, but could I ask you to consider my role and pay? If, within 2–3 months, you feel I've earned it and the company can afford it, I'd be very appreciative. But if not, I completely understand." That's polite. It doesn't corner them into a yes or no. And you've gently appealed to their ego, because you've tied your request to the success of the company. You'll find you get a "yes" far more often that way. And one more thing: keep it private. The quickest way to kill a raise is to brag about it, because then everyone starts asking, and the boss feels trapped.

Now, let's talk about thinking.

What we think is one thing. But how we think, that's what really transforms our lives. We can't always control the thoughts that land in our minds, but we can control how we process them. I made a conscious effort years ago to change the way I think. Instead of letting the natural negative voice take over, I began to reverse-engineer situations. You've probably heard of "reverse engineering" in the field of engineering. I use what I call reverse thinking. Take a goal or desire, then mentally work backwards. For example, how do you become an Olympian runner? I have no idea. But I can reverse-step it back down to my speed. That way, the big dream doesn't feel impossible; you can see the steps in between. When I face a big problem, I don't panic. My first thought is always: there's a solution. That one thought creates hope, even just a little, and it's enough to get me moving. I ask myself, 'Can I solve this?' Do I need help? Do I know someone with the experience to guide me? I brainstorm options, even if nine out of ten are useless, because that one might just be the answer. And I've found again and again: the solution is usually already there. Sometimes, it just takes a week, a month, or a fresh perspective for it to reveal itself. Most people hit one roadblock and say, "Well, that won't work. Too expensive. Too hard." But often it just takes a little creativity.

Like my brother the other week. He rang me and said, "Hey, you gave me an idea. I might be able to buy that waterfront apartment up the coast." It was listed at $1.1 million, and he had $850,000. At first, it seemed impossible. But instead of quitting, he thought differently. He planned to offer $850,000 in cash up front with a delayed settlement of $250,000 over 2–3 years (vendor finance). That would give him time to slowly renovate, add value, and either refinance or sell another asset to cover the balance. Will it work? Maybe, maybe not. But the point is, it's creative and it just might be a win-win. This is why I believe with everything in me that how we think is more important than what we think. A mind that can think differently, ask "how, why, who, when, and where," that's a mind that always finds solutions. And there's always a solution. A "no" often just means not yet. Please don't treat it as a wall; treat it as a speed bump. Timing is everything. A poorly timed yes can cost you more than a well-timed no. Never waste energy arguing with a no. Instead, ask yourself: What needs to change so this becomes a yes? Sometimes "no" is a blessing. It redirects you toward something far better than you originally asked for. The people who get the most "yes'" in life aren't the pushiest; they're the ones who prepare the ground first.

Negative Thinking

Many people suffer from negative thinking and often imagine the worst possible outcome. I'm not sure why some lean that way, but I do know this: what we read, listen to, and surround ourselves with has a massive impact on how we think. That's why, at times, I just switch the media off. It's often so negative that it starts to poison my mind. Instead, I'll watch or read something uplifting, true stories about underdog sporting teams, people overcoming adversity, or even a good love story (as long as I'm not single during a breakup,). One of my favourite proverbs is:

"Do not be conformed to the pattern of this world, but be transformed by the renewing of your mind."

That verse has shaped my life. Because let's be real, patterns conform entirely to most people. Popular trends. Fashion. The latest "cool" idea. Even their finances. Many live paycheck to paycheck, buying the big house, the shiny car, the "look at me" lifestyle, while broke every month. That's not transformation, that's entrapment. I decided I didn't want to conform to the mindset of just being an employee. Nothing wrong with employment, I was one for years, but I knew it wasn't my destiny. I didn't want to conform to debt-driven living either. Instead, I chose to renew my mind and think differently.

That's part of why I'm writing this book: to help others see there's a different path. Now, don't get me wrong, I still enjoy a nice car or a nice watch. But I don't buy them to conform or prove something. I buy them because I can, and because I enjoy them. The difference is motivation. It's funny how people struggle when you don't conform. Say you don't drink at a party, and suddenly, you're the odd one out. People will say, "Oh, there's nothing wrong with having one or two." Sure, but there's also nothing wrong with not having ten or twelve. I'm not against drinking; I'll have a couple occasionally. But when I don't, I don't feel pressured to join in just because "everyone else is doing it." That's sheep thinking. It's the same with cigarettes. Years ago, smoking was the "cool" thing. Now, most people avoid it. Vaping has just become the new conformist habit; it's cheaper, doesn't stink, and people do it anywhere. But that's the point: culture shifts, and people shift with it. Rarely do people stop and ask: Am I thinking for myself here, or just conforming to the crowd?

Influence

I learned early on how powerful our actions and attitudes are in shaping how others perceive us. In year 7, my first year of high school, I was about 13. I was usually a B student, maybe a C if I wasn't interested. But I had an English teacher, Mr. Wilson, and we hated each other. At the end of the year, students were graded on a scale of 1–10 (1 being the highest), plus A–D for effort and behaviour. I got a 10DD, the absolute worst. And I knew I didn't deserve it. Maybe the D for behaviour, but not the rest.

That grade stuck with me. The following year, I was constantly in trouble and had to carry a report card where my teacher signed off on my behaviour in every lesson. If one were bad, I'd be in detention and banned from sport (as a rugby league player, it was devastating). So, I made a decision. I sat at the front of every class, did my work, shut up, and behaved. As a rough football player, I also controlled the classroom. If kids misbehaved, I'd just turn and say, "Stop," and they would. The week before reports, I was joking with my teacher, "A 1AA would be great, Miss." When reports came out, I couldn't believe it: 1AA.

That taught me a life-changing lesson. I didn't deserve 10DD the year before, and I didn't really deserve 1AA either. The truth lay somewhere in between. What got me the upgrade wasn't intelligence. It was behaviour. Respect. Politeness. And the willingness to change my actions. Teachers and bosses are human. They get angry. They get spiteful. They reward kindness and punish arrogance. Mr. Wilson was an immature teacher, and my grade was unfair. However, the next teacher taught me that respect and relationships can have a significant influence on how people perceive you. And that's true in life. We'll all have "Mr. Wilson's" bosses, clients, colleagues, and teachers who seem dead set against us. Fighting them rarely works. But influencing them? Adjusting your attitude and actions? That can change the game completely. Sometimes, the best way to overcome negative thinking isn't in our heads, it's in our actions. Respect, kindness, and self-control renew more than your mind. They renew your opportunities.

Negative Thinking

Your inputs shape your outlook. What you watch, listen to, and read becomes the fuel for your thoughts. Don't conform, transform. Just because "everyone does it" doesn't mean it's right for you. Respect changes results. Politeness and humility often open more doors than raw talent. Actions influence perception. Your behaviour shapes how others perceive you. Stop feeding negativity. If media, people, or habits pull you down, switch them off. Year 7 taught me this: you can't always control how people treat you, but you can influence how they see you. Negative thinking shrinks options. Positive thinking expands possibilities.

Negotiation

People think negotiation is all about clever words or hard-nosed tactics. But here's the truth: you can't negotiate with someone who's too emotional. If the person dealing with you is angry, frustrated, or fired up, your first goal is not to win the argument; it's to calm the storm.

Emotions First, Logic Later

An angry person is usually irrational. They're not listening to reason, and they're not thinking clearly. In that moment, throwing facts or deals at them is like throwing fuel on a fire. Instead, lower your tone- Answer gently- Actually listen to what they're saying. Sometimes, just being heard is enough to bring emotions under control.

Defuse Before You get refused.

Your main objective in the heat of the moment is not to "win," it's to diffuse. A soft answer or even a small apology can help alleviate the situation. If it makes sense, ask: "Is there anything I can do to help fix this?" That demonstrates humility and a willingness to cooperate, rather than fight. But if the person is too far gone, shouting, abusive, or completely irrational, don't waste your breath. The most brilliant move is to walk away. "When you're ready to talk, let's discuss it later." Not all problems need to be solved immediately.

The Right Time Matters

The best negotiations usually happen later, when the dust has settled. That's when people can think, reflect, and reason. That's when deals get made. Negotiation is not about overpowering. It's about timing, tone, and creating the right conditions for wisdom to enter the room. Negotiation is not about overpowering. It's about timing, tone, and creating the right conditions for wisdom to enter the room. If you can master that, you'll win more deals, avoid unnecessary fights, and walk away with both the relationship and the result. Most people fear conflict and give away too much too early. The best negotiators ask questions more than they talk.

Negotiation in the Real World

Most people think of negotiation as sitting in a boardroom with lawyers and contracts. But real negotiation happens every single day, when you buy a house, sell a product, win a job, or even ask someone out. And here's the first rule: I don't like the "either/or" game. The kind where someone says, "It's either A or B." Life and money don't usually work like that. Real negotiation is about finding out what people actually need, then structuring a deal around it.

Property Negotiation

If I'm looking at a property, I don't start with "Why are they selling?" even though that's what I really want to know. I lead into it. I might ask: "Is there a mortgage on the property?" If there isn't, it often means they bought years ago and don't need the asking price; they just want the cash. If there is, I'll ask, "When did they purchase it?" That tells me if they're flexible. For example, if a couple bought it only a year or two ago, they probably need every dollar to clear the mortgage. That usually means they won't budge, so I often walk away.

However, one of my best deals came when two elderly sisters passed away, and their six adult children were inheriting the house. I knew that splitting the money six ways meant an extra $5,000 or $8,000 each wouldn't change anyone's life. So, I offered $60,000 less than the asking price, with a

24-hour time frame and a quick settlement. They countered, and I quickly re-countered at $45,000 less; they accepted. Why? To them, it was just a few thousand each, essentially free money. To me, it became a great long-term asset.

(((((((dad story))))))) no2

It had been about three years since Dad "won" the lotto, well, he thought he did. By then, he had forgiven me (sort of), so I figured it was time for round two.

Now, Dad's second home was the local club. That place was his church. Every Friday night, the big draw was on: they'd pull a member's number, and if you were there, you'd win a brand-new car. But if you weren't there? Tough luck. No car. No second chances. I set the trap. My daughter-in-law was the perfect accomplice, sweet voice, believable, not the type you'd expect to stitch you up. I told her, "Right, he'll be home about now, give him a ring and go for it."

The phone rings. Dad answers. "Is this Jim ....?" she asks. "Yes, love," he replies. "Well, congratulations! You've just won the car! Your membership number came up just now!" Dad says, "Sorry, love, I'm not at the club, I am around the corner at home."

She doesn't miss a beat. "That's okay, you've got about five to ten minutes to claim it from the front office, otherwise it closes until next week." Bang. Hooked.

Dad shouts down the phone: "Don't worry, love, I'll be there in three minutes!" You could hear the adrenaline pumping through his veins. He was probably already putting his shoes on mid-sentence. That's when I jumped on the line. "Oi, Dad, you're a boofhead! You've been had. We stitched you up again." There was a dead pause. Then a yell. Then a string of words I won't repeat here. Let's just say the air turned blue. He was fuming, swearing, pacing the room. Then, after about five minutes, the storm passed, and the laughter came out, big belly laughs, tears in his eyes. He shook his head and said, "You mongrel. You bloody got me again."

See, the thing is, winning a car would've been cool... but making him think he won a car? That was priceless. Oh, the joy I've brought into my father's life, short-lived joy, sure, but joy all the same. And yes, I'll admit it, I enjoy it too.

Deals Without Cash

Sometimes negotiation isn't about the price, it's about the structure. Let's say something is for sale at $4,200, and I already have a buyer lined up to purchase it from me for $5,500. The problem? I don't have $4,200, but I have an idea! So, here's how I play it: Offer $3,800 cash upfront (even though I don't really want it at that price), then offer $4,200 with a two-week payment plan. That's the price they ideally want. Most sellers will take the $4,200 in two weeks, because waiting a fortnight doesn't matter to them. By then, I had already sold to my buyer at $5,500, so I completed the deal with $0 out of pocket and walked away with a $1,300 profit. This works for $4,200, $42,000, or $420,000.

"It's not I can't, how can I?"

My Bobcat Business Trick

Years ago, I had a bobcat and tipper business while working nights in a glass factory. People would ring asking for quotes, such as the price to dig out a driveway, etc. Instead of starting with my rates, I'd start with: "What do you need done?" "When are you looking to get it done?" I would clarify and leave no doubt that I can do the job, with no problem. But their answer to (when) was the code - If they said "next week, I knew I had the code cracked there and then - I'd reply, "ok, let me check," and I would then quickly say "would Wednesday work for you... (wait for yes) And before another word is said, I reply, "Wednesday would work for me. I would say, "Great, I've just locked you in for 7 am Wednesday next week," and then, without a missed beat, say politely, "It will only be about $250-$300 max, it's a straightforward job"! As soon as they agreed on a time, the job was mentally booked in.

Now the psychology flips. They've already committed to a date. Saying no becomes more complicated than saying yes. I booked dozens of jobs this way, without ever "negotiating" on price. I recommend that any businessperson read sales books and listen to podcasts. Sales is a part of business, and even in a 9-5 job. You are always selling something. Your time is constantly being sold. Learn how to sell it well and then buy it.

Negotiating in Dating

Negotiation even applies to relationships. Too many people say, "We should catch up sometime." That's vague. It goes nowhere. Instead, be clear: "I'd love to take you out for dinner. Are you free Friday night?" (Specific) - requires an answer.

If she says no, ask for another day. If she counters with, "Not this week, but next weekend works," then you're in business. If there's no commitment at all, take the hint and move on. If she really wants to go out, she will let you know. Pushing will just turn her off.

My advice: Be polite, respectful, and don't push, but be specific and confident. The first outing should be about nothing more than having a fun, relaxed time. Play the long game; kindness goes further than pressure. And let's be real: it's a lot easier if she already likes you, and if (like me) you're an incredibly great dancer. Bingo!!!

Takeaway

Negotiation isn't about "winning." It's about understanding people, structuring deals, and playing the long game. Whether it's property, business, or dating, the same principles apply: Ask the right questions (indirect first, direct later). Structure deals around needs, not just price. Create a commitment early. Be kind, respectful, and patient. However, have a thought-out plan for the questions you will ask and their sequence. Often, we spend so much time on pricing, volumes, and so on, and don't even get to that stage because we're given the excuse. But that's precisely what it is. So, avoid the space for a reason! That's how you walk away with results, relationships, and sometimes, the girl too.

Negotiating for Products & Services

Negotiation doesn't only happen in big property deals or boardrooms. Some of the most significant talks involve everyday products and services that your business relies on. Here's my simple process: Start with one unit. Always begin by politely asking if they can give you a better deal for just one.

Keep it light, even humorous. People respond better to friendliness than firmness. Move to bulk. Once you've got a better price, step it up: "Okay, what if I buy 10?" See where that lands. Scale it up. Then ask: "What if I buy 10 every week or every month?" This shows consistency and loyalty. Suppliers love long-term regular orders. Ask for terms. Next, request a 30-day account to pay, or flip it: "Can you give me a better price if I pay cash upfront?" Both options create leverage. This way, you're not just buying, you're building a relationship with your supplier that benefits both sides. Also, your boss will love you for it too!

"You need money to make money"

Here's a myth: you need money to make money. Wrong. You need ideas, confidence, and negotiation skills. Say you work in a restaurant or bar. You could visit a winery and pitch them- "I'd like to sell your wine to my clients. Discuss the styles, quantities, and your plan to grow sales.

E.g. -Every winery wants more sales. If a bottle sells in a restaurant for $50, you might consider negotiating to buy in bulk at $10 per bottle. Then push further, 100 bottles = $8 each. 300 bottles = $6 each. Once you have the pricing ladder, present it to your clients: 48 bottles are $20 each. 100 bottles = $16 each. 300 bottles = $12 each. You explain: "To get these prices, we need to place the full order together."

Result: you've pre-sold the wine, collected the money upfront, and placed the order, with zero money of your own. Sell 300 bottles at $12, and if you move them for $18, you've just made $1,800 in one deal without touching your own wallet—also, larger margins if you sold a few online - direct sales to the public. And wine is just one idea. This model works with any product.

And remember, I did this with 13,800 bottles per order $0. Down. (Shipping container)

CHAPTER 16

GENEROSITY

"A generous person's world gets larger and larger. "I believe generosity has been one of the most significant factors in my success, not because I have to get, but because giving always opens doors. Let me be clear: I can't stand TV evangelists who prey on desperate people with prosperity scams. I once heard one say, "God has told me if you give $5,000, He will heal you." I wanted to smash my TV. It was manipulative and cruel. That's not generosity. That's abuse. Real generosity is different. It's giving because it's right, and yes, I've seen it come back many times in my life.

Example 1: $1,000 seed, $11,000 harvest

About 20 years ago, I owed $10,000, but I didn't know how to pay it. I had about $2,500 at the time. Instead of holding on to it tightly, I donated $1,000 to a cause I believed in. In the weeks that followed, I landed a Bobcat job worth $2,700, and I received a $900 tax return. A few other unexpected amounts came in. By the deadline, I had $11,000 in my bank. Coincidence? Maybe. But I've seen it too many times to dismiss it.

Example 2: The $60,000 mentor

Years later, I took over a business with 25 staff and had to cover wages. A mentor of mine, unprompted, deposited $60,000 into my account to help. Why? Because he'd seen me live generously before, even when I didn't have much. I immediately sent back $30,000, saying it was too much, and repaid the rest soon after. He didn't want it back, but I wanted to honour him. That man has been one of my closest friends and mentors for nearly 20 years. Alex.

Why teach being generous before making money? Firstly, it is a law – you reap what you sow, be gracious and generosity will come back to you. Also, if you learn to put others before yourself, then you will be able to prioritise asset building and Wealth building. The tightest people I've met are not the wealthy, as one might believe. The most kind-hearted and generous people I've met are often wealthy because they understand the value of generosity. I know two brothers, who gave $1,000,000 to a charity/foundation, and they are very successful developers. They don't have

113

$50 million sitting in their bank accounts either. Well, they might? But they are both generous men.

Chuck Feeney (The "Secret Billionaire" Who Gave It All Away), Co-founder of Duty-Free Shoppers. Made billions but lived modestly, wore a $10 watch, flew economy, and didn't own a house or a car. Secretly gave away more than $8 billion to causes like education, health, and peace efforts. By 2020, he had given away his entire fortune, retaining only about $2 million for himself and his wife. His motto: "Giving while living."

Andrew Carnegie (The Steel Magnate)

One of the wealthiest men in history. Famously said: "The man who dies thus rich dies disgraced." Gave away about 90% of his wealth ($350 million at the time, equivalent to billions today). Built over 2,500 public libraries and funded schools, universities, and scientific research.

Takeaway

Negotiation and generosity may sound like opposites, but they're really two sides of the same coin.

Negotiate hard on deals and structure them smartly

Be generous with people, time, and resources. One grows your wallet. The other grows your world.

There are actually three sides to a coin - the edge, the face, and the back. Most people don't even realise or think about it. We usually say a coin has two sides, but it is so obvious: there is one small, full-round side, but often we can't see it, just like the opportunities right in front of us. If you don't know how to spot them! You can't find what you don't know you're meant to be looking for

The Power of Generosity

One of the most generous people I know is my younger brother. He left school at 15. He was always in the bottom classes, rarely attended school, and spent most of his time skipping classes with his friends. On paper, you'd never predict success. But he had one thing: he could sell. He started out hustling in sales, Optus phone plans, then automotive paint, then street light poles. One day, his opposition in Melbourne asked him to be their agent in Sydney. They offered the same salary, a car, and 15% commission. He asked me what I thought. I asked him: "How much revenue did you sell this year?" He said: "$6 million." So, I asked: "If you went out on your own, how many of those customers would stay with you?" He said: "At least 20%." My answer was simple: "That's a no-brainer. Do it!"

Within a year, he was making $300–400k with almost no overhead, just one employee. However, there was a catch: his supplier in Melbourne consistently sent him defective or missing poles. Customers grew frustrated. That's when I reminded him of the Chinese guy he'd once helped set up as a quality-control officer for his old company. I told him to reach out. Stay loyal to Melbourne for the big contracts, but start doing small ones on his own with proper quality control. His primary concerns were quality control and ensuring cash flow for the orders. That was the turning point. He imported his first shipment; I loaned him the money (he paid it back within weeks), and today his company is one of the largest in his industry in Australia. He could lend me money now without a second thought.

Quiet Acts of Generosity

But here's the real point: despite all his success, he's one of the most generous men I know. When one of our family members was suicidal and out of work, he told him, "Move back to your hometown. I'll cover your salary and rent until you get back on your feet. And again," When my son volunteered as a youth leader on a small salary while studying at night, my brother paid his rent for two years. Quietly. Nobody knew. I didn't hear these stories from him; I heard them through another brother who was the middleman. That's real generosity: giving without recognition.

Generosity Is Acceleration

I've seen it again and again: people accelerate in wealth when they are generous. It's a law, what you sow, you reap. This week, I've been under pressure, dealing with health concerns, accounting problems, and GM issues. Stress everywhere. But one of my best mates is also going through a divorce, struggling badly. So, every day this week, I've been taking him for coffee, lunch, or just a drive along the beaches, making him laugh. Because generosity isn't only money, it's your time, presence, and care. Be generous with your time, and time will be given back to you in ways you never expect.

That's why I refuse to sow gossip, discord, or drama. Life is a harvest, and you always reap what you sow.

Joy in Giving

There's no better feeling than giving someone a gift, seeing joy in their face, or even a tear rolling down their cheek in gratitude. It changes you. Even the wealthiest know this. The late Kerry Packer, one of Australia's most iconic businessmen, once won big at a casino. He asked the woman who had been serving him all night how much was left on her mortgage. Then he paid it off, in full. Not all wealthy people are tight-fisted misers. Many are generous. Sure, some get tax deductions. But let's be honest, you can get tax deductions for buying toys or turning holidays into "business trips." The difference is in the heart.

The Lesson- Wealth and generosity are not opposites. In fact, they feed each other. Greed shrinks your world- Generosity expands it. And the people who live generously not for show, but quietly, behind the scenes, are often the ones who accelerate the fastest in life.

Billionaire friend

I remember a young friend of mine, Jono. Quiet, shy, tall, white as white can be, and bald. He was Swiss, waiting on his visa and unable to work. He had no money of his own. His wife, on the other hand, was short, dark, and Filipino, a senior manager at a large corporation, earning a substantial income. They were a hilarious pair together, yet a perfect match.

One day, Jono came to me almost in tears. He said, "I feel bad because all my wife's friends, and the people I know, are so generous and kind. And I want to be like them, but I have no money at all." I turned to him, smiled, and said, "Jono, you are a billionaire." He looked at me, confused. "What do you mean?"

I said: "You are a time billionaire. You have more free time than anyone I know. You should become the most generous person with your time. You don't need money to be generous; generosity is a heart thing, not a material thing. You can be generous with your words, your actions, your hospitality, and especially with your time. If you live that way, trust me, soon you'll find other areas in your life where you can be generous too. And in time, money will be the least of your worries." Years later, he has become very well set up in life.

My goal was always to build assets so I could become a time billionaire!

Generosity Is Heart, Not Wallet

That's the truth: I haven't seen many generous people become poor from it. But I've seen generous poor people who ended up living blessed and abundant lives. There's an old reading that says:

"Give, and it will be given to you. A good measure, pressed down, shaken together, and running over, will be poured into your lap. For with the measure you use, it will be measured to you." Imagine if more of us lived that way. When I mentor younger men, this is often the hardest lesson for them to grasp. They think generosity is about having plenty first, then giving it away. I tell them the opposite: start with generosity, even in the most minor things, and plenty will follow. For example, if you're out with generous people, the kind who happily pick up the big bills at fancy restaurants, don't just sit back all the time - Step up and cover the smaller ones. Pay for coffee. Shout a cheap lunch. Even the smallest gestures are noticed, especially by wealthy individuals. It shows your spirit, not your bank account. Because in the end, generosity isn't about what you have in your hand. It's about what you carry in your heart.

CHAPTER 17

DISCIPLINE

Discipline is one of the most underrated attributes in life. We should discuss it further and, more importantly, put it into practice. We often look at people and are amazed at their achievements. Take Olympians, two of the most significant events: the 100m sprint and the men's 100m relay swim. I've watched documentaries on these athletes, and I can honestly say I could never commit to their level of work: the training, the diets, the early mornings, the late nights, the studying, the research, all for the tiniest improvement, a fraction of a second, a few centimetres.

Their commitment and discipline are extraordinary. But here's the thing: that same discipline, when applied to marriage, work, friendships, business, and even our own attitudes, creates equally powerful results.

When starting a business, you need to be fully committed like an athlete. Research, prepare, and conduct thorough research. Passion is not enough. I've walked through shopping centres and seen new shops where I know, just by looking, that they won't survive 3–5 years. Why? Because passion doesn't equal profit, and discipline in research was missing. Too often, people invest hundreds of thousands into shops that never had a chance.

Discipline also applies to health. I love sweet food and snacks, and I've always struggled with sleep. So, I discipline myself in practical ways; I don't buy junk food because I know I'll raid the cupboard at midnight. I make sure I train 2–3 times by Thursday, so I only have one more session to go by Sunday. Some weeks, I'll even train twice a day. Over the past 5 years, I've lost 15kg and kept it off. My daughter is also disciplined: whenever she gains 2 kilograms, she diets until it's gone. She's a wife, a mother of two, and a full-time worker, but she's disciplined, and it shows.

Discipline as Freedom

Discipline initially appears to be a limitation, but in practice, it creates freedom. For example, if you discipline yourself to save money, you're free from debt; if you discipline your mind with focus, you're free from distraction. If you discipline your body with exercise, you're free from an ugly boyfriend ;)

Discipline Builds Compounding Results

Most success in money, relationships, or health isn't built in one big moment. It's built brick by brick, day after day.

Discipline is the quiet force that keeps you laying those bricks when motivation fades. Motivation starts the engine, but discipline drives the car.

Discipline is Self-Respect

Every time you follow through on a promise you made to yourself, you strengthen your identity. When you break discipline, you don't just lose progress; you chip away at trust in yourself. Discipline is how you say to yourself: "I matter enough to keep my word." Be honest, if you said to yourself, I'm going to do... start a great business or buy a nice home! Would you really believe it? The point is, when you do believe in yourself, you will do it, your behaviour and choices change because you know it's happening once you sacrifice and commit. Try it!!!

Discipline vs. Desire

Desire says, "I want it now." Discipline says, "I want what matters most." It's not about suppressing desire; it's about training it, aiming it, and choosing wisely which ones deserve your energy.

"Discipline is the bridge between goals and accomplishment." Everyone has goals. Few have the bridge. Discipline is what makes the difference between dreamers and those who do.

Our Words & How We Treat People

"Sticks and stones may break my bones, but names will never hurt me." One of the biggest lies ever told. Words matter. They shape lives. I often notice how people interact with those around them, like how they treat Servers, security guards, and cleaners. Are they respectful? Grateful? When I semi-retired, I volunteered and helped clean offices for a mate. The staff didn't know who I was- to them, I was just the toilet cleaner. How someone treats you when they think you're "unimportant" reveals their true character. Kindness costs nothing. Respect costs nothing. A simple "thank you" or handshake can make someone's day. And apologies, they're powerful too. Saying sorry doesn't guarantee forgiveness; that's a gift.

But apologising clears your heart and shows humility. I've also learned not to speak in anger. When frustrated, I now go quiet, because words spoken in emotion often become regrets: it's better to have fewer words and less regret. The way we talk to those closest to us also matters. We'd never say to our boss some of the things we say to our partner. Imagine the worst thing you've ever said at home; if you said that at work, you'd lose your job instantly. So why do we let our families bear the brunt? Discipline with words matters.

Words can build up or tear down. Praise what you want to see more of, and compliment publicly when someone goes above and beyond. Speak life into people. I often tell my sons they are competent, because I want them to grow into that truth. I'll even joke with strangers, telling women how lucky they are to have the "most handsome man in Sydney" beside them. It makes people laugh, but it also spreads positivity. And it's not just how we speak to others, it's how we talk to ourselves. "I'll try" is a weak phrase. It's a get-out clause. I prefer: "I'm in." "Let's do it." Go all in. Even if it fails, you gave it everything.

Selling vs Keeping Assets

I'm a big fan of holding onto assets, especially real estate, rather than selling. Unless a deal is simply too good to pass up, I'd much rather refinance, tap into the equity tax-free, and keep the asset. As long as the new loan is positively geared, I'll hold it for the long run. But selling a business is a whole other story. But sometimes life forces your hand.

During my divorce, I owed the ATO around $300,000 in tax. Painful. I kept them at bay for as long as I could, making monthly payments to demonstrate that I was doing my part. Eventually, though, the ATO was patient but firm; it had to be paid. Thankfully, one of my assets had grown from $900,000 to $2.2 million during that period. I refinanced it, cleared the debt, and continue to see million-dollar gains. If I hadn't been disciplined, I might have panicked earlier and sold under pressure for far less.

That's the key lesson: understand tax and play the long game.

Employees get taxed the hardest. Business owners have more options. And minimise their taxes - Investors and company owners have even more if they're disciplined and educated. That's why people like Elon Musk can show almost no income on paper, yet create billions in value. He doesn't sell, so there's nothing to tax. It's the same with property. If your investment goes up $300,000 in value, you pay no tax until you sell. Is that unfair? Not at all. If the government doesn't refund you when the value drops, why should they tax you before you realise a gain? The system rewards those who understand how it works.

And let's be honest, governments waste more money than anyone. I've seen it firsthand. Departments blow their leftover budgets at the end of the year so that they don't lose funding the following year. Millions wasted, year after year. I've had departments approach me with ridiculous requests just to burn money before deadlines. It's a broken system. If governments rewarded efficiency the way private businesses does with bonuses for savings and incentives for innovative management, billions could be saved. But instead, waste continues.

The wealthy understand this game. They don't think about money the same way most people do. They're not necessarily smarter, but they know the rules. They cracked the code, and they understand that you use debt to get wealthy, not to look rich.

- **Golden Rule: Only** sell if the money from the sale will go into something that gives you a higher return or solves a significant problem (like wiping out a tax debt). If it's just to "cash out," think twice - what if you kept it for another 8 years and it doubled?

- **Refinance Before Selling:** Banks will often give you equity on the increased value of a property without selling it. That means you can access cash tax-free while still keeping the appreciating asset. Ask Two Questions Before Selling: What will I do with the money? Will that use of funds create more wealth than keeping the asset? If you can't answer "yes" to the second one, keep it.

- **Beware the Lifestyle Sell:** Many people sell an asset to buy a car, a boat, or a holiday. That's spending wealth, not building it. Use assets to fund assets, not liabilities. Forced Sales Are Lessons: If you ever have to sell under pressure (divorce, debt, health, etc.), don't beat yourself up. Learn from it, reset, and make sure next time you're in a stronger position. Wealthy Thinking: Wealthy individuals rarely sell their most valuable assets. They leverage them. Middle-class individuals often sell too quickly because they want to appear wealthy today, rather than being wealthy tomorrow.

People-

Do you see their name or title? See a person, not a problem. See their name, not a label. Every person has a story. Every person has a gift. And every person has a friendship they can offer.

Something I try to do is look down, look up, and look sideways, meaning, I notice the people around me. I don't look over someone's shoulder for a more "VIP" face while I'm in mid-conversation. Have you ever been mid-sentence and they suddenly glance past you, wave at someone else, and break the flow like you don't matter? I no longer get offended, but I also don't bother finishing either. I just turn, start talking to someone else, and leave them to it. People like that won't build long-term friendships, because they'll likely do the same to the next person.

When I go out, my goal isn't just to hang out with my friends (though I do, and we have a great time laughing). It's to talk to the Uber driver and ask about his family. To ask the waitress her name. To thank the staff at my table every single time, even if it's the seventeenth. A smile, eye contact, and respect cost nothing, but go a long way. We all have a gift, and it isn't truly a gift until we give it. That's how we make our suburbs and cities a little happier, one person at a time.

I'm not afraid if someone ignores me or doesn't want my friendship. There are people I don't want to be friends with, either. But what if my small hello cracks their hard shell? Many people wear masks, appearing unapproachable, but I'm thankful that others over the years have helped open me up and bring out the friendly person inside me.

I remember meeting Graham. He was the softest, kindest, most polite man I'd ever met. He was open to everyone, shared stories, and had this gentle way. At that time, I was young, hard, and angry. Over the course of a couple of years, he softened me. I was meant to be him and learn from him.

In Sydney, you see homeless people with makeshift beds, trying to stay warm, sometimes asking for money. It's easy to think, "Go get the dole, get housing." But who knows their story? It's sad to see in Australia, but many have lost so much hope that they've even given up on help. I hope I'm never in that position, but at the very least, I can say hello. Remember: they have a name and a story. Most people don't care how much you know until they know how much you care. Being authentic and genuine is the only way to build trust, love, friendships, and relationships.

And here's one of the biggest lessons I've learned: listening is more powerful than speaking. Too many people just wait for their turn to talk. You can see it in their body language; they're not really hearing you, they're just waiting to pounce. That kills the connection. Proper listening often means you don't even need to say what you were planning to say; the point gets through naturally. In the past, I dominated conversations out of ego, driven by a desire to impress. These days, I try to say less. Sometimes silence is smarter.

The point of conversation is to connect, not to show off. Using big words that hardly anyone understands doesn't make you intelligent. I look at it like this - they are trying to impress the listeners with their vocabulary, it's like men who work out at the gym, and when they speak publicly, they like to flex and have their arms in the flex position. It cracks me up. It's as if they are overexcited about their achievements, or perhaps a touch of insecurity. Real intelligence is simple. If people can't understand and apply what you say, what's the point?

I've waited for conversations to pause, and my line is: "I like big words too, like wheelbarrow." :)) That usually gets a laugh, but it also makes the point: don't try to sound intelligent. Be intelligent, and communicate clearly.

Quick Connection Hacks

Remember names. Nothing makes someone feel more valued than hearing their own name. Smile first. A genuine smile disarms people and makes you more approachable. Ask, don't tell, questions open doors. Statements close them. Notice the unnoticed. Thank the cleaner, the security guard, or the barista. They're often invisible to most. Pause before replying. It shows you listened, not just waiting to speak. Look people in the eye. It builds instant trust. Leave people better than you found them. Even a small compliment can shift their day.

Unknown-Author

The Man Who Hid His Name

There was once a man who painted on walls but never signed his name. When the city was asleep, he crept through the alleys with cardboard stencils and a spray can. He worked quickly because he knew authority hated truth more than paint.

Other artists chased fame, selling their names for fortune. But this man stayed hidden. He mocked the powerful, exposed the greedy, and drew flowers in the hands of soldiers. People tried to erase him, but the more they erased, the more he seemed to appear. Soon, his art was everywhere, not just on walls but in hearts. His works sold for millions, though he never asked for the money. The world called him Banksy, though no one knew who he really was.

The lesson: Sometimes the strongest voice is the one that doesn't seek applause. By hiding his name, he made his message louder.

When we set aside our ego/fame/fortune, there is something attractive that makes you stand taller than everyone else in the crowd, as most people are seeking relevance. When someone could be famous but chooses not to be, it's as if we almost want to ensure they get credit because they don't seek it. What do you want to be famous for? What value does it really bring you? If not money, what is the point?

I remember talking to an influencer, a friend of a friend, one night, and she was famous. She looked great - in fact, The Daily Telegraph did a full-page feature on her about being an influencer and the fame that came with it. I didn't know her apart from being friends with my friend. I think people can gain a following in certain circles and feel like they are famous. Still, outside that bubble, they are relatively unknown, as I wish to be. She told me she couldn't afford to pay for an Uber to her photo shoot the next day; she had to take a train. I'd rather be Neville nobody and have some money to pay for an Uber. They would rather be broken and famous, not having to work? I just don't get it. Years later, she chased a wealthy man in Europe, I heard.

It's funny, men just don't do this - I don't mean this nasty or rude, but look at Rich - super rich women who are not beautiful and not skinny (no, I'm not saying fat and ugly because I'm not shallow Hal), a lot of men chase youth and beauty, I guess. Some women prefer money. I've been asked many times why I want money. I don't - I want to live and enjoy life, not work. To

124

do that, you need assets, not money. Means to an end! I know a guy well who has a decent social media following. His thing is about depression, but my ex-partner wouldn't follow him as it was so dark/depressing and negative, and I said to him Why don't you put some positive stuff and talk about some wins in your life. He replied faster than a kid chasing an ice cream truck. It doesn't get traction, likes, or go viral. He didn't care; he just wanted to be famous.

Well, I just burst out laughing, and it cracked up. I said 'Fair enough,' so I stopped offering advice and suggestions. I'm totally fine if someone wants to be famous, but it adds zero value to their life. If playing that game brings you happiness and provides a lifestyle you enjoy, allowing you to live a fulfilling life every day, then maybe.

But imagine being extra famous, you can't just walk around and enjoy life like a normal person. I think part of the purpose of life is simply being regular and flowing in and out of crowds, people, and events. I question fame - the desire: why would you want actually to be famous? So, people bother you and don't really care about you, but they want a selfie with you to post and look famous for 5 minutes. Everything you do wrong is scrutinised and shared with everyone. Famous people often seek privacy and quiet places, avoiding crowds. I've chosen to do most of the things I do in privacy with business coaching and mentoring privately, and invite only, and I choose who I work with. I don't advertise or pursue clients. I sometimes prefer to have a piece of the pie, pending the type of coaching and business, then charge a fee of $10k or $20k. (Asset over cash) – Chasing fame isn't going to improve my life. Some of my famous friends can't enjoy the simple things we do every week, and when they do, they are extremely careful about what they do and who they are with in public.

Writing this book just enlarges my platform with privacy; who knows, things may change in the future.

The Best Investments I Ever Made (And You Can Too)

When most people hear the word "investment," they instantly think of stocks, property, or crypto. And sure, those are valid. But the best investments I've ever made weren't always financial; they were foundational.

When you build a house, any builder will tell you that most time and effort goes into the foundation. Because if that's wrong, the whole structure fails. Life is no different.

These are the kinds of investments that made everything else more profitable. They paid me for years, changed how I thought, and protected me during storms. Let's talk about them, not just to inspire you, but to equip you to make the same kind of moves.

I Invested in Thinking Bigger

I used to think small. I believed rich people were just lucky, or maybe dishonest. I thought success was for "other people." Then one simple word from a mate changed my life. He said, "Add a zero." He told me to add a zero to my monthly goal. And straight away, something clicked.

Now, I know you want to hear about the deals, but it's like telling someone how incredible a Brazilian BBQ is (I'm actually going to one at my mate's place Wednesday night, he works with us). Imagine if we pulled out a frying pan and said, "Ok, show me." It doesn't work like that. You need open fire, coals, smoky wood, flames; it's a whole different setup. That's what thinking bigger is like. You need the right fire before the meat even hits the grill.

So, I invested in myself. My mindset had to change, radically. Not because I was dumb, but because we have all been taught the wrong way to think. Honestly, I believe half the time it's deliberate.

Here's what I invested in: Books- Mentorship- Time in reflection and jotting down thoughts (I don't "journal" in the fancy sense, but I write down ideas, solutions, even great jokes). Books, especially, have been my secret weapon. They've given me knowledge, skills, and wisdom that give me an unfair advantage in business and life.

Sometimes I know how to price or negotiate a deal, not because I'm guessing, but because I've learned how to ask the right questions without asking directly. People often give away information if you know how to listen, and books taught me that.

So, here's my advice: don't just read, apply. Don't just highlight a line and say, "That's nice." Use it. Something I've realised is that people will pay big money (including myself) if you can save them time or solve a big problem. For example, I've helped save, clients $200+k per year or increase their business substantially, and to pay me a small 10% of that is worth their investment. Also, saving people time and energy is very valuable when their time is limited and expensive. People want solutions and real help, so find solutions and answers for people and increase your value.

CHAPTER 18

BOOKS THAT CHANGED MY LIFE -

Now don't get weird on me. It's a book inside the Bible called Proverbs. It's not religious, it's wisdom, straight-up wisdom on dealing with people, money, and life. There are 31 chapters. I try to read the one that matches the date; it's the best book I've ever read for relationships and life in general.

Rich Dad, Poor Dad

This one cracked open my understanding of assets vs. liabilities. Simple, practical, life-changing.

ChatGPT (yes, I'm serious), I use it like Google on steroids. You can ask about anything. Elon Musk once said there's no need for university anymore because the internet can teach you more than any university can. Big call, but I get it. That's the first investment: thinking bigger. Get your mindset right, and everything else -money, business, relationships, levels up.

You Can't Build Wealth with a Poverty Mindset

One of my favourites and most exciting investments wasn't money; it was teaching my kids. When they were still living at home, I constantly drilled into them the basics I'm sharing in this book. They grew up understanding the difference between an asset and a liability very well. When each of them finished school, I made a deal with them- They could live at my home rent-free. If they saved half their salary, I would provide them with their first car and a fuel card. If they didn't work and instead went on unemployment benefits, their board would equal whatever the government paid them in benefits.

Safe to say, they never went on government benefits. And now, I'm proud to say all three of my kids own two or three positively geared properties each. That came from saving half their salary, applying what they'd learned, and marrying partners who joined in with the same mindset.

I believe investing in other people is one of the most significant investments you can ever make. There's an old saying: "The best way to learn is to teach." When you teach teenagers, you quickly realise you have to explain things very simply. That skill has stuck with me. I believe that whether you're teaching, inspiring, or negotiating, you should use simple language that anyone can understand.

When people use big words to try to sound intelligent, they actually do the opposite. They demonstrate their ignorance and lack of wisdom by failing to share a good story or lesson. Knowledge is not the same as having wisdom. One builds up life, the other just puffs up ego. An educated person without wisdom is like a grand piano with no one to play it.

And here's a surprising fact: the people with the highest percentage of bankruptcies aren't poor. They're actually university and college graduates. Knowledge without wisdom can lead to financial ruin.

Investments That Paid in Lessons

Some of the best investments didn't pay me money; they paid me clarity. I've learned as much (if not more) from failed side hustles as I have from the big wins.

One expensive lesson was when the GST (tax) was first introduced. I bought an industrial block of land. The contract said the price "included GST." That meant I thought I could claim back 10% of the purchase price, basically, cash straight back into my bank account. For example, if you bought a property for $200,000, you'd expect to receive $20,000 back in GST.

So, I submitted my claim. However, the government flagged me as a potential fraud. I wasn't. The problem came down to two small words in the contract: "if any."

It stated that the price included GST, "if any". This meant that if GST was legally required, it was included. But in this case, it was clever wording on their part, and an expensive mistake for me. Back then, GST was brand new. If you'd bought land before GST came in, you could choose to sell without GST. I didn't know that. My solicitor didn't either. And because of that one phrase, I lost thousands.

It was my mistake; I should have researched GST more thoroughly, especially in the context of commercial real estate. It hurt, but it was one of those lessons you only need to pay for once. And even today, the same trap is possible if you don't read contracts properly.

Some investments pay in dollars. Others pay in wisdom that saves you thousands later. Both are worth it.

I Invested in Learning How Money Actually Works

Most people think money is a dollar note in their hand. It's not. That $50 note- It's not even worth five cents. It has no value in itself.

Money is just a currency, and currencies are only valuable because we, the taxpayers, agree to trade with them. They're not backed by gold like the US dollar once was. The government prints it (or now, creates it digitally), but here's the kicker: every dollar printed is actually a loan from the central bank.

That means all the "free money" floating around, including the handouts, the grants, the stimulus, comes with a price tag: debt + interest.

Inflation Isn't an Accident—It's the Plan

Here's the truth most people never realise: inflation isn't just "something that happens." It's built into the system.

Every time more money gets printed, the money already in circulation loses a bit of its power. That's why your savings in the bank quietly die every single year.

Think about it like this: if the US. The government owes $30 trillion. Do you think they're rushing to pay it back? Not a chance. They don't want to wipe the slate clean; they just want to service the interest and keep the machine ticking over for 20 years. Their real plan is to make that $30 trillion debt feel like just $5 trillion by inflating it away. Here's how it works: Government income rises through growth, higher wages, and, of course, higher taxes. Inflation erodes the real value of debt. The dollar slowly loses purchasing power, but tax revenues explode.

Let me show you with simple numbers:

When I was about 20 years old, the average weekly income was around $260, and the average tax bill was $30. That meant the government was making $30 per person each week.

Fast forward 30 years, and today the average income in Sydney is more like $1,500–$2,000 a week. The average tax? Around $600 a week.

That's a massive jump in tax collected from each working person. And here's the kicker: the government didn't really "do" anything extra to earn that. Inflation and wage growth did the heavy lifting. The debt they were terrified of back then now looks like pocket change compared to the flood of tax money coming in.

Multiply that across an entire working population, say 150 million taxpayers in America. If each person used to pay around $50 a week in tax, but now pays $300 a week, suddenly the government's tax income goes from peanuts to billions upon billions. That's how they plan to service massive debts: borrow now, devalue the money later, and let inflation and immigration swell the tax base.

Of course, the risk is always there; if the currency crashes, the whole game collapses. But until then, governments play this system like a fiddle.

Example: You've got $100,000 in the bank. Inflation runs at 3% (and that's the official number; real life often feels more). That's a $3,000 hit to your money every year, without you spending a cent. Over the course of 30 years, that $100,000 loses about 90% of its value. Think about it: 30 years ago in Australia, $100,000 could buy you a beautiful home. Today? You'd be lucky to get a mailbox.

For example, my brother lives in Double Bay (double pay); his apartment is a large 4–5-bedroom unit with some water views, worth approximately $4.5M if he had bought it when he was born. $100,000. If he still owed the bank $100,000, who cares? His repayments would be nothing. So, the payment on the debt, unpaid since 1975, of $96 per week ($100,000) in 2025, is still unpaid. Therefore, the old debt is okay. Harmless - in 2025, to buy it, repayments might be $6500 a week.

Same property - see the difference in inflation and devaluation of the dollar. This is how Governments see debt. However, if it grows too large too quickly, it collapses. Even if it owes that $100,000 in 10 years, it is likely worth $9M. Who cares $96 a week.

That's why I say: inflation isn't an accident, it's the plan.

Ok. You can have option 1 or 2.

1.- $1,000,000 cash in your bank today, or 2. A property - currently valued at $1,000,000.

Which do you want to own in 20 years? For example, the interest and inflation on average $1M. It would likely be around $1.7 million with interest; we can only buy 30% of that house now. The property would be approximately $5.5M, and we would be 70% better off with the property.

How to Beat the Inflation Game

Own Assets, Don't Just Save: Cash loses value. Property, businesses, and shares tied to real companies usually rise with inflation.

Use Debt the Smart Way: Inflation Hurts Savers but Rewards Borrowers. If you've got a loan on a house or business and inflation eats away at the value of money, you're effectively paying the bank back with cheaper dollars. Think Long-Term, Not Short-Term: Governments think in decades. Don't panic about the news today; ask where values, wages, and taxes will be in 10–20 years. Invest Where People Must Spend: Housing, food, energy, things people can't avoid. Inflation pushes these up, and if you own them, you benefit. Remember the Pattern: Governments borrow, inflate, and tax more. You can either fight it and get crushed, or play the same game on a smaller scale, owning assets, using leverage, and holding for the long haul.

Why Saving Alone Won't Save You

Most people are advised to save 10% of their income for retirement (superannuation, similar to a 401(k). They rely on compound interest, thinking it will save them. But here's the problem: Compound interest grows your cash. But inflation eats your money faster.

That's why the average person retiring in Sydney today might have $300,000–$500,000 in superannuation. Sounds like a lot, right? However, with the average income in Sydney now ranging from $100,000 to $150,000 a year, that's only 3–5 years of salary to live on, for the rest of their life. Some wages are significantly lower than $150,000 a year in Australia, but they typically reside within a 1-hour drive of Sydney. Incomes in other countries are considerably lower. No wonder people feel trapped. They worked their whole lives, but they never learned what money actually is.

A Simple Newspaper Lesson

I bought the Telegraph newspaper in Sydney today. It cost me $3.50. Five years ago, it was $1. Did the newspaper suddenly quadruple in value?

No. It's still the same paper, the same ink. The truth is that our dollar has devalued. Your money buys less and less every year, not because products have gotten better, but because we keep printing more currency and creating more debt.

Why Bitcoin (and Other Limited Assets) Attract People

This is one of the reasons Bitcoin is so popular. Unlike dollars, it has a limited supply. Once all the coins are mined, that's it; no more can be created. Whether you like Bitcoin or not, the logic behind it is sound: people are looking for something that can't be endlessly printed and devalued like government currency.

Why Superannuation (401k) Is Flawed

This is also why I believe superannuation is highly flawed. If you're putting 10% of today's income into super, by the time you retire 30–40 years later, that money will be worth a fraction of what you thought it would be. What appears to be 10% today may feel like 1% in the future.

It is essentially betting your entire retirement on the long-term value of cash holdings. And history shows, it doesn't. It's better than nothing, but so is a donkey if you don't have a car to drive.

Money Is Debt. Debt Is Money.

Once you truly understand this, the light bulb lights up. Money is debt. Debt is money. They're the same thing. But here's the catch: there's good debt and bad debt. Most people use only bad debt, such as credit cards, personal loans, and car loans. That's why they spend their whole lives working for money instead of making money work for them. Good debt, debt that buys you income-producing assets, is the game changer.

Why Schools Never Teach This

Ever wondered why schools, colleges, and universities never teach this? If everyone understood how money really works, most of us wouldn't keep working our whole lives in jobs we don't like, just to pay off debt and save into a system designed to shrink. The truth is, your first and best investment isn't property, shares, or even a business; it's knowledge. Once you understand how money really works, you'll never look at your savings account, super, or government handouts the same way again.

Money isn't what you think. It's not about paper or numbers on a screen. It's about value, inflation, debt, and wisdom. Learn this first, or risk wasting decades of hard work.

I invested in Learning from People Who Were Ahead of me.

One of the smartest things I ever did was simple: I asked questions. I became a sponge. If I met someone who'd mastered something I hadn't, I asked them how. I valued advice from men and women who had achieved real success through wise choices and hard work. Schools never taught this stuff, and with no disrespect to hardworking teachers, how can we expect them to teach what they've never been taught themselves, or what they haven't personally achieved? So, I asked questions, a lot of them.

Sometimes it was a tradesman who'd built a thriving business. Sometimes a salesperson makes great money. My younger brother built his entire company around sales, and I learned a great deal from him. He devoured books and podcasts and spent time with old-school salespeople who just knew how to deal with people and close a deal. In my early days, I was fascinated by the real estate industry. I'd ask questions to anyone who owns two or three houses. One thing stood out: wealthy people either made their money in real estate or parked their wealth in it.

So, I thought, if they're doing it, I'd better too.

From Residential to Commercial

Initially, I followed the standard path: I purchased a few residential properties. But then I realised there was a better game: commercial property.

The returns were higher, the capital growth more substantial, but the risks were bigger too, especially with vacancies. After conducting some research, I discovered that the commercial property type with the lowest vacancy rate is self-storage units. The second-best option was another category I'll cover later, but self-storage became my primary goal. (Don't worry, keep reading, my friend :))).

Still, real estate taught me something crucial: it provides capital growth and a modest cash flow. But the big money, with the best tax benefits, is in businesses. That's when I shifted.

CHAPTER 19

BECOMING A CURRENCY BREEDER

Once I understood cash flow, leverage, tax strategy, and compound growth, I stopped chasing money. I wanted to become what I call a currency breeder.

I wanted my money to make money. My assets to make money. My companies make money. Because here's the truth: working for money is the slowest, hardest way to build wealth. Money is simple, but not easy. Learn the rules, and you'll stop being a slave to them. Once you've got a bit of understanding, you start to create your own rules. You build your own game. And then you invite others to play your game, like the BUCK and DOE story.

There's a saying: Lenders are the head, borrowers the tail. Learn how to be the head.

The Head, Not the Tail

I no longer see myself borrowing money. My assets borrow money. My companies borrow money. They do the work; I just structure it. I picture my wealth like a flowchart or puzzle on a whiteboard: it has to be simple, clear, and structured. Not small, but simple. That shift, from "I borrow" to "my assets borrow" is enormous. It's a complete mindset flip. And where did I learn this? Straight from the first book I recommended: Proverbs. It says, "First establish your vineyards, and then build your house." In modern language: "Prepare your work outside; get your career ready, and after that, build your house."

Most couples today do the opposite. They move in together, borrow to the max for a house and car, and get stuck in debt for years. The proverb says, "Build income first." Add assets, properties, and businesses, then build your dream house.

What If You're Maxed Out Right Now

If you're already maxed out, don't panic. You'll be fine. However, you need to change your mindset. Step 1: Eliminate liabilities one by one: car loans, credit cards, big mortgages. Clear them. Got a car loan? Rent the car out on a daily/weekly basis. Or sell it. Got a mortgage? Rent out a room. Airbnb it in peak season and stay at your parents' place (don't tell my kids this). Got equity? Restructure the loan and negotiate for a lower rate; even a 0.5% reduction can be beneficial. And if you're a little more advanced, you can get creative. Here's an example: House worth: $800,000- Loan owing: $600,000

Bank charges: 5% interest ($30,000 a year, $577 a week)

You sell the house on vendor finance (you become the bank). Sell price: $830,000 Charge 6.5% interest (because you're the lender + seller) Buyer pays: $53,950 a year ($1,037 a week)

Now look at the shift: Your mortgage costs: $577/week- Your new asset earns: $1,037/week- Net profit: $460/week ($1,842/month)

You've just turned a liability into an asset. Yes, it's legal. Yes, it's done often. And yes, people run whole companies around this.

There Are Always Solutions

See how easy it is when you shift your thinking? Perhaps you could sell the house and free up $200,000 for a better investment in real estate. Maybe you restructure. The point is: there are solutions.

The only question is: are you creative enough, or desperate enough to find them?

Because here's the truth: when you get momentum, your brain starts coming up with solutions. And when you're hungry enough, or forced to, you'll push until you find one. Some people will tell you, "You can't." And they're right, for them. They can't, because their financial vision is too limited. But you can. Just ensure you have a reputable solicitor, the correct contracts, and the necessary caveats in place.

And be careful who you share your dreams with. Sadly, some people are ignorant, harmful, or just financially low-IQ. Others? Well… let's just say they're window lickers. (joke)

Lesson: Find people ahead of you, learn from them, get creative, and never stop asking questions. You don't need to reinvent the wheel. You just need to be smart enough to ask the right person how they rolled theirs.

I Invested in Real Estate

My first property wasn't flashy. But it paid me while I slept. Rent came in, the mortgage payment went down, and the value increased. Then I bought another. And another.

Real estate provided me with passive income, capital growth, and leverage to scale up. And just as importantly, it gave me something priceless: a sense of control over my future.

Lesson: Real estate won't make you rich overnight, but it will make you wealthy over time.

Adding Value, the Simple Way

What I love about property is that you can buy it for less than it's worth if you know how to negotiate, be patient, and remain firm. And then you can improve it and add value yourself. One place I bought was $50,000 under value. Then I- Added a double carport- Turned the garage into a lounge room and an extra small bedroom- Put in a new kitchen- Painted the roof- Cement-rendered the old orange bricks- Built another double carport in the backyard and walled it in as a BBQ/games room- Knocked out a wall for a big open-plan living area- Painted the entire inside.

I picked up cheap bricks online (with a weird colour, but who cares, cement render hides it). I bought standard-size carports (6x6m and 8x6m) and had a tradie install both in a day.

Total improvements? About $25,000. If I'd gone the expensive route, custom carports, fancy new kitchen, paying tradies for everything, it would have cost closer to $80,000. The result? The property's value increased by over $200,000 in just 12 months. We paid $155,000, spent $25,000, and within a year, it was worth over $375,000. Two years later, I sold it for $580,000. Today, it's probably worth around $900,000.

Here's the kicker: if I had my time again, I wouldn't have sold it. Don't sell, refinance if you need cash.

Why Real Estate Wins

You can't do that with shares. Property is hands-on, flexible, and simple to learn. Even being a half-qualified tradie (or with mates who are), you can do a lot of the work yourself for cheap. The other secret weapon? A good broker. Get one who deals with multiple lenders. They'll not only find you the best rates, but more importantly, flexible loans that free you up to finance the next deal. I've never chased the cheapest rates; I wanted the best value and flexibility to grow and re-borrow many times over.

The Simple Formula for Real Estate Wealth

Buy under value (be patient, negotiate hard). Add improvements (renovate smart, not fancy). Revalue the property (force the equity up). Refinance (pull some cash out without selling). Repeat (roll profits into the next deal).

Lesson: With real estate, you don't just wait for growth; you force it. Buy under value, add improvements, refinance, repeat. That's the wealth cycle.

I Invested in My Own Ideas

There came a point where I realised: I can't just work for someone else's dream.

I had a senior manager who was a complete jerk. I didn't trust him one bit. To be honest, he actually inspired me to be self-employed, funny how life works like that. My uncle was the head union boss at the time (good and bad for me), but he exposed this guy for the brown-nose grub he was :) Sorry, delete that. Ever since, that manager has hated me. So instead of letting him have power over me, I decided to take the power back.

I started making deals, stacking cash, and launched my first two businesses: Bobcat and truck hire, and self-storage units. That's how I got control of my life. Started a side hustle- Launched a product- Packaged my knowledge. It didn't take off overnight, but it gave me confidence. Eventually, it provided me with a cash flow. And then? Freedom.

A Simple Freedom Formula

Here's one of the strategies I like to use (and I've actually done it). They say in real estate, the law is: every 8 years, property doubles in value. Let's be conservative and call it 10 years.

Now imagine this: Buy 5 to 8 properties, positively geared, at say $500k each. Sit on them. Let them grow. After a few years, those $500k properties are worth $750k… then $800k… then $900k… and so on.

Now here's the trick: Refinance one property each year for $100k, tax-free -Live off that $100k while the properties keep growing.

Example:

- **Year 1:** Property 1 – bought for $500k, now worth $750k, refinance $100k tax-free.
- **Year 2:** Property 2 – worth $800k, refinance another $100k tax-free.
- **Year 3:** Property 3 – worth $850k, refinance $100k.
- **Year 4:** Property 4 – worth $900k, refinance $100k.

Do this in rotation, and with eight properties, you can comfortably live off $100k a year tax-free for over a decade, while your assets keep growing in value.

Fast forward 13 years:

- Each property is worth $1.2m
- You owe $600k on each one
- That's $5m+ in capital growth
- Plus, now you can refinance $200k per year tax-free

And the best part? You never sell, so you never pay tax.

Creativity Creates Wealth

Yes, it takes work to find positively geared properties. And yes, most people will tell you it's impossible. They're right, for them, because they don't see what's possible.

But you're going to!

There are always deals out there. Sometimes you need to look in another town or city. Sometimes you need to add a room, a granny flat, or convert a garage. Worst case? Rent out rooms. Not glamorous, maybe messy, but it's a start.

The point is: your most significant asset will always be your mind, and the creativity inside it. Creativity turns a simple property into a dual-income asset. Creativity finds opportunities where others only see problems.

"It's not I can't, but how can I? "

I Invested in the Right Relationships

Here is an old proverb, a warning, and wisdom:

"Wealth brings many new friends, but a poor man is deserted by his friends."

Meaning: money itself isn't love, but it attracts connections and people. Use it wisely to build meaningful ones, not shallow ones. And realise why some people want to be around. This one is underrated. The people around you either: Fuel your fire or smother your flame. I stopped spending time with complainers. I look and find people who are going where I want to go. As you grow, this circle slowly changes, but some are for life. Mentors, peers, and even books became part of my circle. They inspire you and even push you to great heights, inspiring new beliefs.

One of the things that impacted me significantly was when I began to realise what was truly possible for my life. Like when my mentor Alex encouraged me to "add a zero" to the dollar figure I was aiming for per month. Once it really became a part of my thinking, it opened up my mind to investments and deals I would never have even considered. At first, it seems a little out of reach, but one small win at a time, and one big deal you manage to get over the line, it all adds up. Without that belief, you may never even attempt it. My income increased, my vision became more apparent and sharper, and I stopped doubting myself. My assets started to grow and become more profitable. Now I've added another zero to my monthly goal.

I hear people say "get a dream," and that's fine, but only if the dream isn't a fairy tale. It has to be something you believe in, are attempting, and are aiming towards.

Lesson: The right people multiply your momentum. The wrong ones drain your energy and maybe even your destiny.

I've been through this a few times in my life. I'd get new friends who were fun and exciting for a while, but then I'd realise these relationships weren't contributing to my well-being. They weren't aligned with who I wanted to be or what I wanted to do long term. So, I'd slowly pull back. Sometimes I allowed limited time with them, other times I cut them off entirely if the influence was negative.

I Invested in Space, Down Time

This was one of the most essential and overlooked investments I ever made. I stopped overcommitting. I created time buffers. I gave myself space to think, rest, and grow. People underestimate downtime. Doing nothing. No schedule, no plans. Take a moment to rest and let your mind relax. That's when ideas come.

Sir Winston Churchill said that some of his best ideas and strategies came to him when he was at rest, smoking a cigar, and doing nothing. Brainstorming groups are great. Reading and studying are great. But never underestimate what's inside your own mind. One thought, combined with another, fine-tuned over time, could be the answer to a genius idea. The problem is, most people use their "thinking time" to worry. To imagine what could go wrong. But that time can be used to create, challenge your own thoughts, and grow new ideas. And maybe your idea on its own is average. But combine it with a couple more thoughts, or with someone else's insight, and suddenly it's a big one. That's how empires are built.

Do you really think Facebook, Instagram, Spotify, or Virgin came from just one guy sitting alone with one thought? No way. Yes, one person often gets the credit, but reality is different. There were always other partners, thinkers, advisers, and investors shaping the idea. So don't just build your own pie, get other people to help bake it. I'd rather own 5% of Facebook than 100% of a small computer shop.

Think big. Own a small piece of a big pie. But be careful with whom you join. That's another story, but it's a big one.

Facing the Unthinkable

The past two weeks have been a challenge, involving scans, blood tests, ultrasounds, and an MRI. I was waiting for Wednesday to see the specialist. My doctor was very concerned that I may have prostate cancer.

Then yesterday, I woke up with a sharp pain behind my right shoulder blade. I'd had this pain before, usually lasting twenty minutes or so. However, this one continued to worsen as the day progressed. By night, I couldn't even lie down. It felt like someone was stabbing me under the shoulder blade. I'd also noticed shortness of breath the past couple of weeks. And in that moment, my worst thoughts hit me: Oh no, not again. Years ago, I had a life-threatening blood clot, 11 cm long, sitting right before my heart. If it had broken loose, there was no coming back. It was over, red rover. This pain felt similar. But I had a dilemma. My appointment the next morning could be life-changing, a cancer diagnosis. Do I risk missing it? Or do I risk dying overnight from a clot? By 2 a.m., the pain was unbearable. I knew I was in serious trouble. So, I went to the hospital and told them, "I think I have P.E. (pulmonary embolism)." I'd had it before. I knew the signs. After scans and 9 hours, the doctor sat me down. "Well, you probably already know," he said. "Yes," I answered. My worst fear was confirmed: a large clot, 2 cm from my heart.

So here I was sitting in a hospital (not a plane), knowing the danger of blood clots, and in five hours also facing the possibility of a cancer diagnosis.

And you know what? I smiled.

Choosing my outlook, I've been through rough seasons: I've been shot- I've been stabbed- I've been in jail- I've been divorced. But this? This just felt surreal.

On top of that, my dad's wife is about to die from cancer any day now. My dad himself is declining with cancer. And now I had to find the right words to tell my kids, my partner, my father, and my close friends. But one thing is for sure: I now have plenty of downtime to think, write, and pour myself into this book. And weirdly, I'm excited. Excited to market and promote it in ways nobody's seen before. Excited to dream up crazy ideas with my sons, they're wild when they're together!

See, sitting around sad isn't on my agenda. My brain doesn't work that way anymore. Yes, I may be in a hospital bed, but I don't see myself as part of that picture. I see a future that is bright, adventurous, and full of new ideas, new friendships, and lessons still to come.

What Really Matters

The truth is, knowing my heart is right with God is the best feeling. That's my foundation. But I also see the world around me. Leaders and politicians are more obsessed with popularity and power than with truth and the well-being of their people. That concerns me. But I also believe in a generation rising above it, a generation led by conviction, vision, and purpose.

And here's what I see coming- A shift in women's leadership—not driven by anger, equality movements, or quotas but by justice, conviction, and genuine capacity. Young men are learning to lead not with aggression or arrogance, but with strength, humility, and respect. A balance of masculine and feminine leadership that complements, not competes.

I don't see men and women as equals in the sense that they're the same, because they're not. But I do see strengths that are unequal but complementary.

My sons have strengths that my daughter doesn't. However, my daughter possesses leadership, compassion, and ambition that many men will never have. And this generation needs both. Younger men no longer respond to the old-school, harsh leadership style. They need strong leaders with vision, but also leaders with compassion and care. That's why we desperately need women to rise alongside men. And when that balance happens, we'll see the kind of future we dream of.

CHAPTER 20

MONEY

Okay, let's get that saying "money is evil" out of our vocabulary. That comes from a misquoted verse: "the love of money is the root of all evil." Not money itself. Big difference. Money in the right hands can do extraordinary things. Without money, we wouldn't have hospitals, nurses, libraries, and let's be fair dinkum, the NRL and NFL football to watch! I've already discussed good debt and bad debt, but here's another layer: years ago, the U.S. dollar was backed by gold. That meant the U.S. could only print as much money as it had in gold reserves. That gave it real value. It's why the U.S. dollar became the world's standard, especially in the oil trade.

However, President Nixon subsequently removed the gold backing. The dollar became just another currency. No longer backed by gold, but by U.S. taxpayers. Since then, they've been printing it like Monopoly money. That's why inflation eats away at it every year.

Think of bread. Once 50 cents. Now $4. Did bread get better? Did it gain superpowers? No. It's the same bread. The currency just keeps losing value.

What Money Really Is

At its core, money is simply a medium of exchange; it replaces barter, allowing us to save and transfer wealth. A measure of worth is a tool to value goods and services. That's not evil. That's helpful. Here's the truth: money won't change you. It will just amplify what's already inside you- If you're greedy, money will make you greedier. If you're generous, money will multiply your generosity. If you live in fear, money will fuel it. If you live in abundance, money will open even more doors.

It's not money that's evil. It's often what people are willing to do for it.

The Good in Money

Freedom & Options- My favourite currency is time. Money buys options, mobility, and space to pursue calling, creativity, and contribution.

Imagine having two spare weekdays off, because your assets covered your income. You could:

Volunteer at a women's refuge- Help in a youth outreach- Coach a local sports team, or simply take more holidays

That's freedom. Money helps people take control of their lives, especially those born into poverty or disadvantage. It can be a tool for justice and equality when used correctly. Money enables us to care for our families, support causes, and build a lasting legacy. In the right hands, it multiplies goodness. I once watched a podcast about a politician who secretly donated vast amounts of his own money to help people and never advertised it, never seeking credit. That's real generosity. One of the first things I teach friends is this: be generous. I had a mate who never shouted a round, never paid for lunches, and always skipped his share. That mindset alone will keep him broke. Generosity builds wealth, not just financial wealth, but opportunity.

I see my life like a warehouse, not a storage unit. Things flow in, things flow out. That flow keeps creating more. But if you clutch too tightly, stingy with money, stingy with generosity, you'll be stingy when investing, too.

A Lesson from My Mum

Here's a personal story.

My late mother lived on government benefits most of her life. At one point, the government offered her the opportunity to purchase her housing commission home for approximately $85,000. It was worth around $220,000 at the time. I told her, "Mum, buy it. If you're short, one of us three boys will help." But she was nervous. She said, "What if I can't afford it? What if the lights go out, or the taps leak? I'd rather not."

About a year later, I told her that her home she was renting still was worth around $350,000. I said, "Mum, if you'd bought it, you could have sold it today for a $250,000 profit. You've got to put yourself in a position to be blessed." That's the truth: if you sit on the sideline, you'll never score a try.

She never changed. She died in that same home, still struggling.

Tough Love

It's the same with government benefits. I've had relatives who refused to work because they didn't want to risk losing their benefits. They thought it was an entitlement.

145

I told one relative, "That's the whole point, your income is meant to outgrow the benefit." Another old schoolmate once said, "I get paid today." I asked, "Oh, you got a job?" He said, "No, government payment." I said, "Mate, that's not getting paid. That's welfare. Don't call it wages." Sounds harsh? Maybe. But it's tough love.

I have no sympathy for healthy people in Australia who refuse to work. The government already gives enough to eat, drink, and smoke. If it were up to me, I'd ban benefits from being spent on alcohol and cigarettes. Many would suddenly find work.

Because the truth is this: laziness is expensive. And taxpayers- people like you and me are footing the bill. I know this life because I grew up in it. But even as a kid, I wanted out. That's why I was so firm with my kids. I told them, "If you ever go on benefits, I'll take the money off you for board." (And I would've too!) Thankfully, all three are now adults, working hard, independent, and never having to live through what I went through. That's a cycle broken.

Final Thought

Money isn't evil. It's neutral. But in the right hands, it becomes one of the most excellent tools for freedom, empowerment, provision, and generosity. Don't let misquotes or small thinking rob you of seeing what money really is.

Motivation, Growth & The Dark Side of Money

Motivation & Growth -The pursuit of earning isn't just about cash. Done right, it drives discipline, innovation, and problem-solving. Think about technology. Not that long ago, people didn't even have hot showers at home. Today, with the flick of a switch, lights are on, water is hot, and life is easier. That didn't happen by accident. It came from motivated people who refused to quit. (Thanks, Mr. Edison, for not giving up on the light bulb!)

Money, in the right frame, fuels growth. It motivates people to solve problems, create solutions, and build a better future.

The Bad Side of Money

Greed & Corruption- Money can become an idol. Greed drives people to exploit, hoard, scam, or manipulate. Crimes, wars, and betrayals can be traced back to it.

Here's the dangerous part: greed doesn't just trap the foolish. It can blind even the wise. Smart, educated people still fall victim to scams, not because of a lack of knowledge, but because greed has dulled their judgment. Never underestimate greed. It's cunning, persuasive, and always whispering, "just a little more."

Fear & Scarcity

On the other hand, financial difficulties can instill fear. The obsession with not having enough leads to anxiety, mistrust, and selfishness. Comparison fuels it: "How much he has vs. how much I have." Pointless. It steals joy, peace, and perspective.

Identity & Money

This might be the most dangerous trap: confusing net worth with self-worth. That's where pride, insecurity, and shame live.

I've seen it mostly in men. They chase cars, watches, houses, not because they love them, but because they think those things validate them. Sometimes it's even fake watches, fake designer bags, fake sleeve tattoos. Wear it for a few months and make sure it's what you really want. :) I guess.,

The point is this: when validation comes from others, it can also be taken away by others. If your self-worth is tied to applause, position, or status, you're on shaky ground.

My Story of Identity

Years ago, I was in leadership training with three other men. We were being considered for certification as leaders in ministry. I was already leading 50+ men in my business, doing well, and financially far ahead, but I didn't care about a certificate. The senior leader pulled me aside and said, "Two are ready. A third, Gary, really needs this for his confidence. But I'm not sure. You may have issues (meaning with authority). I laughed and said, "I agree." Not sarcastic, genuine. I told him, "I'm not here for recognition or paper certificates. I'm already certified in my heart."

He had nothing to say. Why? Because his power over me was gone. I didn't need what he thought he could give me. In fact, that put him in a dilemma. If I didn't care about his certificate, it devalued it. Eventually, he signed me off, but I never even picked it up. The truth is, my identity doesn't come from titles, salaries, or certificates. It comes from knowing who I was created to be.

Money, Power, and Responsibility

Money is often used to dominate, silence, or enslave. You see it in global politics, in corporations, and even in families. It can manipulate nations, topple governments, and keep people trapped in cycles they can't escape. Power, threats, and wealth often work hand in hand.

However, don't be misled into thinking this only happens to the rich and powerful. The truth is that more crimes are committed in poorer neighbourhoods for financial gain than in wealthy suburbs. I've noticed something else: some of the stingiest, most selfish people I've met have been middle or lower class. At the same time, some of the most generous people I've ever met were extremely poor.

I remember travelling through India and China. Families with almost nothing, people who struggled to get by, would empty their cupboards to host us. They would serve food with pride and honour, even when it meant going without.

These meals, eaten in the humblest homes, remain some of my most precious and unforgettable memories. It is hard to come back to the Western world and complain when you've seen generosity like that. We live surrounded by wealth, convenience, and opportunity. There is nothing wrong with access to wealth, nothing wrong with achieving and obtaining it. But here's the problem: many people in other nations don't have that access. They can't simply "work hard, save a little, and build a better future." The system isn't built for them to climb. Now, I'm not responsible for fixing all of that. Neither are you. However, I am responsible for what has been entrusted to me. And so are you.

We can't do everything. But we must do something.

Unknown-Author

Lesson:

Money reveals the heart. In the wrong hands, it controls, manipulates, and enslaves. In the right hands, it feeds, builds, and blesses. The question isn't how much we have; the question is what we'll do with what we've been given.

We can't fix the whole world, but we can steward what we've been given.

The generous people I meet, who opened their small cupboards and opened their hearts, were proof that generosity doesn't come from abundance; it comes from character.

That's the point: money can't give you identity, and it can't take it away.

Final Thought

Money is a tool. It can motivate growth and progress. But it also tempts greed, fuels fear, and twists identity if you're not careful.

Your job is to master money before it masters you.

Money: Is it a crime to accumulate a lot of it, or waste a lot of it? Not having access to make it certainly is

Lesson for my kids: taking money can be a bad idea!

I often taught my kids lessons about money, positively geared real estate, and how to deal with difficult teachers. I respect teachers, and I can only imagine how hard it must be to teach this generation of kids. Mine were probably either the funniest to teach or the most annoying. All three of my kids have two or three positively geared properties each and are relatively young, 29-33. And they have had these for a few years. And I never gave them cash. I've mentioned that I gave them their first car and provided them with fuel cards. My daughter had the best one out of the three. ;) only female in our (my mother's) family for years. Anyway, I remember testing the three of them while on a family holiday at Coffs Harbour. Lovely coastal town in NSW, Australia. I had some hot green Wasabi on a spoon. Just enough to make your eyes water and your nose do weird things. I said to my eldest son-$5 if you eat this (they all knew what it was) $5 was like $15 back then. My eldest said yes without hesitation, and I gave him the $5. (Eyes watering and not good-his mother wasn't laughing) I asked my second son the same, and he said, 'Just give me the $5 and put his tongue out.' And I gave him the $5.

(Same drama) I asked my youngest daughter, and she laughed, saying, 'Dad, I'm not that desperate for $5.' She looked at her brothers with disgust, almost, so I smiled and said, 'Here's $20 for not being so silly.' The boys began to get upset and angry. I just laughed and said, 'Well, boys, learn from your sister.' Because girls may be more emotional and caring, but often a lot smarter.

I need to describe my three kids (adults) to appreciate some of these stories - they were all champion swimmers, beating millions. Well, just before they got wedged inside their mother's egg, they were.

My eldest son

Either his teacher's favourite or they despise him- No in between. He has a small circle, but a loyal bunch for life. He played professional football for a bit, then took over my company. He was too good-looking to play NRL - hard to get into his circle - but he is one of my best mates. Great at business and creative, and is going to be five times what I am. He has two personalities 1. Quiet. Polite and professional. 2. After four beers. Loud. Funny (he thinks he is), talkative, annoying - he might be a comedian or a ballerina, confusing? And the second-best pool player in Australia and the second-best arm wrestler I know.

My second son

He is knowledgeable, genuinely in the top 3% of our state when at high school. (his older brother would say 'state of confusion'), And because of that, he asked me cheekily if he was adopted. I laughed and pointed at him and said, 'Seriously, son, who would adopt that?' Haha. He is one of the kindest man you will meet, but he could have been a UFC fighter. Those two traits don't usually mix - I remember when he was 15 and in year 10, the year 12 boys were 17-year-old boys, and one of the older boys beat up his little Asian mate. Hence, my son went and asked them to leave his mate alone, and then one of them tried to beat my son up, but he got beaten up instead. Then his bigger mate came over to sort my son out, and he also got beaten up by my son. I had to go pick him up, and he got a week's holiday from school as a result. At 15, he was known to be the toughest kid in his school and town, but he later became a quiet churchgoer and settled down. Luckily. Champion guy. He was the 5-year-old kid who said firtyfree (33). I explained that there is no such thing as Firty firr ... I tried to explain.... - the next day he asked about the milk in the thiridge (fridge). I had to explain again.

My sons together are hilarious. At every party we have, they bring out a guitar and free-style sing, teasing everyone and anyone who dares to interrupt them.

My baby daughter - nothing to say except 'favourite/perfect' (my sons will read this and laugh, saying, 'Yes, true, haha'). She is a great mum and works very high up in a bank in Australia - she's super hardworking and resourceful.

CHAPTER 21

THE LANGUAGE OF WEALTH

Every industry has its own lingo. Carpenters talk about a "four-by-two" (timber). Doctors often use Latin terms that sound like a foreign language. Tradies shorten words, bankers use acronyms, and lawyers bury meaning in phrases the rest of us barely understand. It's a foreign language, until you're inside that world. Then suddenly it makes sense.

Money and wealth have their own language, too.

When people truly understand finances, they communicate in a specific way. They employ terms, ideas, and phrases that may sound unfamiliar to the average person. And here's the truth: if you don't learn the language, you won't understand the system.

Hearing What Others Can't

I was reminded of this recently when I had an ultrasound. Pregnant women get them all the time, but here's what it actually is: a high-pitched sound our natural ears can't hear. The machine picks up the echoes and translates them into something we can see.

Finances are similar. To some people, financial conversations bounce off them like inaudible noise. It doesn't register. They plod along, maybe even work in the finance industry, but they don't really "hear" it. Their frequency is too low.

Meanwhile, those who have tuned in can pick up what others can't. They hear opportunities. They understand risk. They are familiar with the language and can quickly determine whether a deal is worth investigating. It may not be your love language, but you need to learn it.

Two Worlds, Same Room

This is why, sometimes, when I discuss investments or financial strategies, people look at me blankly. To them, it sounds impossible or unbelievable. They'll say: "You can't do that."- "That doesn't work anymore."- "Maybe years ago you could, but not now."

And they're right, for them. Because they haven't tuned into the frequency, but for those who've learned the language of money, what seems impossible to others is everyday reality.

It's like living in another world, even while standing in the same room.

Learning the Language

Here's the good news: anyone can learn it. But it requires humility. You have to admit you don't know, be willing to study, and be open to being taught.

You don't have to know every industry's lingo. But if you want to succeed in real estate, business, investing, cafés, tech, whatever it is, you need to learn that language until you're fluent. Only then will you be able to spot opportunities and filter out the noise.

Lesson: Money has a language. If you don't learn it, it will sound like noise and nonsense. If you do, it will unlock opportunities invisible to everyone else.

++ **An update on my health.** Still in the hospital but slowly getting better, this is my second time having severe blood clots in my lungs and close to entering my heart. 30% of people die from it, and I was one of the worst cases they had seen. They called my family from interstate to basically see me, possibly for the last time, and the first time I had it, I had clots all over my body everywhere. They had to put a steel cage in my main artery to keep the clots away from entering my heart after they sent a vacuum tube up through my main artery and tried to retrieve as many of the clots as they could. Still, there was an 11cm clot hanging over a thing called a saddle, and two-thirds of it was hanging just above my heart, and if it came apart or dropped, it was game over. So, I'm now a couple of days in and on blood thinners, so each day makes it much safer and less likely of a tragedy. My doctor and nurses at the Royal North Shore Hospital in Sydney have been excellent. At this stage, I'm not even concerned about the cancer because this blood clot is a minute-by-minute thing. My doctor asked me this morning if I would sit in on a class with his students to discuss P.E. (including blood clots, etc.), answer questions, and assess my comfort level. I said I would love to.

Perspective

Already, I can see the benefits and how this season in my life can help and inspire others. So I went to the meeting, and they were asking about the symptoms and what made me come to the hospital, and how I knew or assumed I had PE again. I explained to them, only because I had experienced it before-8 years ago, that I knew or had an idea. Then, later today, I began thinking along these lines in a general sense: that our past experiences can help us understand what is to come. Our past helps us understand and recognise patterns, situations, or mistakes, and identify things to avoid or make changes before it's too late or a disaster occurs. I avoided being in a serious and more life threatening situation this time around because the first time I had blood clots I went to emergency at a hospital in South western Sydney but because I was unaware of what was wrong and had not experienced the symptoms and pain before I didn't understand what I had and when they sent me home and said it's probably just air pockets causing pain. I took their word for it and went home. This allowed the clots to travel higher up into my body and into my lungs, and further into a place called a saddle, and from there, it drop straight into your heart and kill you on the spot, making it more serious and dangerous than it was this time. Due to the past, I was confident and very direct in what I thought I had and what I wanted them to check for, and these quick actions and choices I made to get to the hospital have definitely saved me from more harm and stress and likely saved my life. The moral is to use your past, whether it's failures, successes, wins, or losses, to help make better and wiser choices. Don't just sit by and allow others to give their opinions, even when they appear more experienced or educated than you. Push hard and don't allow people to assume or be lazy. My most annoying thing is that some companies and organisations have employees who just can't be bothered or don't care to do that extra step, double-check, or seek advice. I almost lost my life 8 years ago because a public servant/employee couldn't be bothered to check properly and investigate just that little extra. Anyway, you get what I'm saying, and my experiences have taught me to push a little and ask more questions to get better information. It may save your business, promotion, or even your life. And remember, there are other suppliers, consumers, and people, and most of all, options from which we can get better service and help. Our loyalty needs to be valued, not assumed, and the opposite is also true - it goes both ways. And I found out I do not have any cancer, just getting a little older!!!

How do you see yourself?

Let me start with this statistic and information. It's mind-blowing, the fact that you are alive and even exist is incredible, a 1 in 300 million chance. There is a greater chance of winning the lotto x52 in a year than being born. So here is why. When your father and mother conceived you, there were between 100,000,000 and 300,000,000 individual sperm cells in a race to get into the egg. And I researched this. Every single sperm is unique and could be a person; every single one of the 300,000,000 of them, added to that, we have 8.23 billion people. Now, what are the chances of your mum and dad meeting? That's a one-in-8 billion chance of them meeting, and also of your grandparents meeting to have them, and then there were wars, famines, and natural disasters. With one hiccup in any of our ancestors, none of us would exist without these miraculous events taking place.

So, the chance and fact that you are even a human and exist is 1 in 10^{2685},000, which is essentially impossible. It has been concluded that actually being born and existing is considered an almost impossible reality. But even just being one in 300,000,000 is incredible. You were the winner - the fastest and strongest of over 300 million. Well done! We are born winners. I think that when we look at it this way, we were born on purpose for a purpose, and you were chosen to be exactly who you are. I don't know what your personal beliefs are, but what a privilege it is even to exist. Now, hopefully, you feel special! I do!

We don't always see reality exactly as it is. We see it filtered through our beliefs, emotions, and focus. Our first step is to change the filter through which we look. Most people's filter is translucent-white; they can see, but they can't really see what's on the other side. Regarding financial filters, we will make adjustments to them during the following few chapters.

This is an interesting topic, and not just seeing, but also thinking about ourselves, is crucial for our confidence and mental well-being.

You and I both were created with purpose, not by accident. There is something in you that this world needs, and no one else can carry it the way you can. This is why I think it's so important to be authentic and be yourself.

Yes, I'm all for growing, maturing, and making positive changes, but not at the expense of trying to become someone else. I like to think of it this way: I want to meet my identical self every five years. I want to be me, and I wouldn't want to be anyone else. But I want to meet a new, refreshed, more creative, and more capable version of myself every five years. I want to grow and become a better, more improved, and upgraded version of myself. "My identical self "

I just asked my eldest son, 33, for this book (seriously), How do you see yourself, and he replied, Well... usually in the mirror. This is the world I live in. :)

We often forget our value when life gets loud and messy. We need to get into the habit of reminding others, but more importantly ourselves, that we (you) have worth beyond a good performance or current circumstances, which is powerful. Seasons in life come and go, and are constantly changing, just as the four natural seasons do. Some seasons are better than others, but always remember that the season you are in now isn't permanent; it's just a season. Your life isn't defined by this moment. It's just a chapter, not the whole story. Don't give up on your future; it's still being edited and written! When people feel stuck, they need hope for what's ahead, not just comfort from what's behind. One of my favourite sayings and thoughts is. "My best days are ahead of me, not behind.

Even during all four seasons, we experience storms, but they can seem dark and daunting. However, every storm I've ever been in has come and gone; no storm in life comes to stay. Let's be real, we all have been through some rough times. You've already survived things you thought you couldn't. That same strength is still in you; it hasn't gone anywhere. You should be proud of the adventures and mountains you had to climb and overcome, even the dark valleys. People often see their weaknesses more than their strengths and areas for growth, but make sure your mirror at home is not one of those weird ones at theme parks that make us look weird and short/tall or wobbly.

Sometimes I wish my friends could see themselves as I see them. You don't have to get it all right and get perfection; you just have to keep showing up. That's what makes the difference in the end. You know that once upon a time, Usain Bolt couldn't even walk; he had to crawl first. Now look at him go! I heard he did okay over 100 m and 200m, and he's not even crawling anymore :) And don't forget, we are all on a journey, continually improving day by day and week by week. Sometimes people don't need more motivation; they need a reminder that they're not doing it alone. Injuries can occur to even the most skilled athletes, and they require rest and recovery time. There is no difference in our lives. Allow time and space for rest and recovery from life's injuries. We all have someone in the background cheering us on. You're built for more than this moment. Don't quit on the seed just because it hasn't grown yet."

Chinese- Moso Bamboo-

It's famous because after planting, it appears not to grow for about five years, but underground, it's developing an extensive root system. Then once established, it can grow- up to about 1 metre per day (sometimes more) during the right season.

We often experience significant growth during the hidden and dark times of life. People might wrongly think you are gone and buried. No way! Maybe you've been planted for a new time, a new season, and a new day, and who knows, maybe the greatest year of your life is about to unfold. Even in silence, growth and movement can occur, sometimes not readily apparent. Don't be concerned about not being seen. Public praise has no value, nor do public negative opinions. What we believe and say about ourselves is more important. Anyway, let's focus on being planted in good soil and not be too concerned about becoming a big, massive tree. Let's get the seed planted first, mixed in a good environment. The tree will be a tree, no matter what people say or think about the seed and its worth. As long as the seed stays planted and doesn't change its mind to become a pumpkin, the tree will remain a tree. Who knows- your **Moso** season might be about to start. Learn to ignore the outside noise and opinions of people who have never achieved much at all themselves. The people who help you get planted in good soil and help water you are the ones we want to listen to and hear from. Not from the thorn bush growing next door. Maybe they have those mirrors from the theme parks in their homes. Because I cannot see how they can look at their own miserable and negative lives and offer opinions to others. I don't give bodybuilders advice on six packs, but I did give my partner advice on being perfect! :)

Lies, Labels versus the Life We're Meant to Live

The Biggest Lies

Some of the biggest lies spoken about us don't come from other people; they come from ourselves. My eyes have seen things. My ears have heard words. My life has gone through experiences that, if I believed them all, would have left me poor, broken, maybe even in prison for good. On top of that, I've even spoken lies about myself. But here's the truth: if I had believed every word I heard, saw, or thought, I would not be living the life I live today.

So, the next time you criticise yourself, pause. Give yourself a break. Allow yourself space and time to grow, learn, and become who you are meant to be. Don't judge yourself on where you are right now; judge yourself on where you're going.

Labels Don't Define You

When I was younger, one of my uncles said about me: "He'll either be in jail or dead by the time he's eighteen." Harsh words. And truthfully, looking at how wild I was, he may have had reason. But labels don't determine destiny.

Yes, I spent weeks in prison once, wrongly accused. Yes, people thought the worst of me. But even that didn't define my future. What defined me was my response: actions, discipline, humility, determination, and the willingness to be corrected. Your current season is not the whole story. Hard times are preparation. Trials accelerate growth. Troubles fast-track wisdom.

CHAPTER 22

WISDOM AND GROWTH

I used to think wisdom came with old age. But wisdom comes from seeking it, listening to advice, receiving correction, and learning from others. It's far quicker and easier to learn from someone else's mistakes than to insist on making them all on your own. Wisdom isn't about being the smartest. It's about being humble enough to learn.

Purpose and Destiny

Imagine standing at the gates of heaven and being shown a video of how your life was meant to be, every promise, every blessing, every opportunity you could have had if you followed your purpose and took courageous steps. Would the person in that video look like you?

That thought challenges me profoundly.

Here's what I know for sure- We were all created for a purpose. Don't let your postcode (zipcode) define your future. We weren't meant to do life alone. Your most meaningful memories always involve people. Relationships matter. Forgiveness isn't optional; it's essential. We all leave a footprint. You may never speak to 10,000 people in a stadium, but you'll meet 10,000 people in cafés, taxis, workplaces, and neighbourhoods. Your kindness and presence could leave a mark that changes their life.

The Power of Simple Moments

I once met an Uber driver who became a close friend. He had gone through a messy divorce, started a small tyre recycling business, then faced health issues that ended it all. He was hurting. But because I took the time to listen, we formed a friendship that encouraged him.

I've met friends in random places, cafés, parties, and hospitals. I've even invited Uber drivers to join house parties (to the amusement of my mates). These aren't "big stage" moments. But they're real, life-shaping moments.

I've spoken on TV, on the radio, and to large crowds. Yet the most memorable and meaningful moments of my life come from one-on-one encounters.

Hardship, Humour, and Hope

Even when I was recently in the hospital with serious health issues, I decided I wasn't going to sit there miserable. I joked with the staff. I encouraged other patients. I made friends. Painkillers probably helped, but I can honestly say I made the most of that week. (home now, much better).

Hardship doesn't have to break you. It can prepare you. Like the saying goes: "Hardships prepare ordinary people for extraordinary lives."

And when I left that hospital, I walked out grateful not just for my health, but for the people who had been part of the journey: doctors, nurses, cleaners, food staff, and volunteers. Every one of them mattered.

Lesson:

Don't let lies, labels, or today's struggles define your future. You were created with purpose. Your destiny isn't determined by what people say, or even what you think about yourself today. You're planted, not buried.

Your best days are not behind you; they are in front of you.

CHAPTER 23

UBER DRIVER

Another story, I was in an Uber one night, and I was talking to him, and he was from India. He was telling me about a customer he had in his Uber one night, and they were discussing his sad situation. He then started talking about cricket. His favourite Australian player was one of our captains, Michael Clarke. The customer said, 'Michael is my friend.' We're going to his house now, and when they pulled up. The customer asked him to wait, and he came back out with Michael. He then encouraged him, said hello, and took the time to speak with him. Now, this Uber driver didn't know that I knew Michael as well, so I contacted him and reminded him of the story. We laughed, and he said, 'Make sure you say hello to him.' You just never know, taking a bit of time to get to know someone, saying hello can make a difference to their day, and it might seem like a small gesture from us, but who knows

The Uber driver mentioned to me when he dropped me off- that after Michael left his Uber, it just put a smile on his face and made him happy for a couple of days. I genuinely don't want this book to be about me, and I think it will be more impactful if I remain anonymous. No, I'm not famous. Just a legend, ha ha.

The "why" behind everything- Universally: Many see meaning in contributing to something greater than themselves, whether that's helping people, leaving the world better than they found it, or fulfilling a spiritual calling.

- **Personally:** It's about what you decide is worth living for, the values, causes, and relationships that make you feel alive.
- **Spiritually:** For some, meaning is rooted in God's plan, divine purpose, or eternal life. For others, it's about creating meaning through love, kindness, and truth.

Having purpose, your personal mission.

All the above points are essential, but this is the real gold. I believe that when we find purpose, it gives us a reason to get up in the morning, and we don't view our lives as simply waking up, working, eating, sleeping, and repeating the cycle over and over.

Purpose reveals meaning. It's the direction you choose for your life. It's usually where your strengths, passions, and impact on others overlap. I found that knowing my purpose gave my life a lot more meaning. It also showed me that there is meaning and purpose even in simple things, such as sitting in a cafe and meeting a random person. I recall reading a book a year ago titled "The Purpose-Driven Life." The basics of it were that we have a certain number of hours allocated in a day - sleep, work, family, and fun. It discussed the importance of maintaining a balance in our lives to accommodate these things regularly, while also making room for other activities such as sports, entertainment, and church. Whatever you do. But we must not allow one or two things to demand too much time and keep the balance.

Once we know our purpose in life, some of these things will naturally fit in or alongside what you do. For example, I was on the radio talking about this, and the host asked me what my purpose was. I hadn't thought about it in a focused way before, nor had I articulated it out loud. Still, I knew straight away, without thinking, that I believe my purpose in life is to help others find their purpose, and it fits into every other part of my life. This included being a father and helping my family find their purpose and discover what they believe they are meant to do. This also helped me decide whether to work with specific companies or not.

Initially, I only wanted passive income and non-time-consuming companies. However, I ended up helping set up and then buy a company that created numerous jobs for the disadvantaged. This company has grown significantly, and now I own it.

. This enables me to assist individuals in advancing their careers and even starting their own businesses.

I have found that once my purpose was clear in my mind and I understood why I was born and put on this earth, it made my future steps and paths easier to see and know what I was meant to do. Writing this book is also another part of this purpose; it all intertwines together. I encourage you to take time to relax and discover your purpose in life; you will be surprised at how invigorating and refreshing it can be.

It answers questions like: Who am I meant to help, and what problems am I here to solve? People with a clear purpose often exhibit greater resilience in the face of hardship, as they view their struggles as part of a larger, more meaningful context. Purpose acts like a compass; even when life feels chaotic, it keeps you moving toward something worthwhile. What is your purpose? No one can tell you, but people can encourage you in the things you are gifted at and unique - that's a good place to start.

The Art of Negotiation

Timing is Everything

Negotiating when emotions are fresh is a recipe for disaster. That's why divorce settlements are among the most challenging negotiations. Pain, betrayal, and emotion can cloud judgment. Picking the right moment is just as important as the words you choose.

The Power of Information

Negotiation isn't about bluffing. It's about knowledge. The more information you gather, the stronger your position.

Take buying a car. The seller wants $10,000. You've only got $8,500. Is it possible? Absolutely. But you need to ask: Why are they selling? How long have they owned it? What do they need the money for?

If they need $6,000 to fund an overseas move, $8,500 cash in hand might be perfect. If they need the full $10,000 for a house deposit, you could offer $8,500 now and $500 a month for three months. It's not always about the sticker price. It's about the why.

Focus on Interests, Not Just Positions

People often state their position ("I want $10,000") but rarely reveal their interest ("I need money quickly to move overseas"). Once you know the interest, solutions open up. The same applies to workplace negotiations: someone says, "I want a raise." But the genuine interest might be, "I feel undervalued." Address the why, not just the what.

Psychology of the Deal

Negotiation is part psychology, part strategy—some timeless principles: Listen More Than You Speak. Silence is powerful. People reveal more than they intend when you don't rush to fill the gaps. (In sales, they say, he who speaks first loses.)- Build Rapport. People are more likely to compromise when they like and trust you. Find common ground early. Ask Open Questions. Try: "What would it take for us to make this work for both of us?" This allows them to own the solution while giving you clarity on the finish line. Stay Calm. If tempers flare, pause or walk away. Negotiating angrily is like driving drunk; you're going to crash. Plan B. Always know your bottom line and what you'll do if no deal is reached. Walking away can sometimes be your most significant power.

And remember: sometimes, not often, but the people across the table really are idiots, and usually, they already know it.

Preparation Creates Confidence

Never walk into a negotiation cold. Know what you want, what they want, and the context in which you're operating. Preparation isn't just about facts; it builds confidence. And confidence communicates credibility.

Win-Win, or Walk Away

The best negotiations leave both parties feeling heard and satisfied. But sometimes, no deal is better than a bad deal.

I've made bad deals before. The day they ended, I was relieved. Not every deal is meant to be saved.

Lesson:

Negotiation is a blend of timing, knowledge, psychology, and patience. The more information you gather, the more options you create. Don't rush. Don't let emotions rule. Aim for a win-win, but always be ready to walk away.

CHAPTER 24

QUALIFIED

I'm not qualified to fulfil my purpose, but my purpose qualifies me for it!

I recall inviting a financial planner to my home when I was in my early 30s. He was from AMP, from memory, and he started the conversation with, 'What age would you like to be retired?' I said 40, and he laughed. He said, 'Seriously, what age?' I knew at this point it was a waste of my time. I find it an oxymoron when someone needs a salary or a wage each week and gives financial advice. In saying that, I know they do have a place to function within society, but probably to sell or recommend products.

Also, I remember a young friend of mine. He was approximately 28 years old, had no money to his name, and was employed by the Commonwealth Bank. He was in control of millions and millions of dollars to make investments and buy shares or currencies. Whatever he was buying on behalf of the members of the bank. I just thought this was absolutely unbelievable. Yet, this financial planner and young employee at the bank, whom you would call qualified, had a degree of some sort. I think my unqualified status has served me fine!

However, I don't think this type of education truly qualifies you for anything except theoretical knowledge. I wouldn't go to a 19-year-old and ask for advice on how to deal with my grandchildren, and I wouldn't ask my grandmother, if she were alive, what clothing I should wear to an event on Saturday night.

I view qualifications in a very different light from being qualified. It's like people who study business management at university, which might be a great subject to study, but it certainly does not qualify you to manage a great business. Years of learning, reading, and gaining knowledge and experience in a business will prepare you to run a business; a university degree will not, but it is likely helpful for an employee. I'm not criticising university degrees at all. There is undoubtedly a place for them, and my son has one; I'm proud of him. However, what he is achieving in life is way beyond the scope of his university degree. Actually, my son took seven or eight years to complete his university degree, not because he's simple, but because he worked two jobs and started building assets while studying at university at night. His life experiences so far have qualified him more than any qualification could, but if you have qualifications, be proud of it.

Almost everyone I know battles with insecurities, self-doubt, worthlessness, feeling 'not good enough,' and not being qualified. I know I do at times. I make a point of not focusing on who I was or even who I am now, but I try to focus on the potential of who I'm becoming and what I will be.

Wisdom-

"Be wise as serpents and harmless as doves."

When I read this biblical passage, my initial thoughts were (serpent) Evil and Trickery, but I knew I had it wrong somehow. So, I did some research and studied up on serpents, wise as a serpent.

A serpent's "wisdom" here isn't about evil or trickery, but about sharp awareness, caution, and strategic thinking. Some qualities that make a serpent "wise"

Cautious and Alert

Serpents move carefully, staying aware of their surroundings to avoid threats and seize opportunities. Wisdom often means avoiding unnecessary danger.

Patient and Calculated

They don't waste energy in constant movement; they wait for the right moment. Similarly, a wise person doesn't act impulsively but considers timing.

Navigate Hostile Environment

A serpent survives even in dangerous territory, adapting to changing situations. Wisdom is the ability to operate effectively even in the face of opposition.

Strategic in Self-Défense

A serpent doesn't attack without cause; it uses its abilities for survival, not random aggression. Wisdom involves knowing when to act and when to remain still.

Blending In When Needed

Many serpents camouflage themselves to avoid danger. Wisdom sometimes means not drawing unnecessary attention until the right moment.

In short, a "wise serpent" in the biblical sense is shrewd without being corrupt, aware without being fearful, and strategic without being deceitful, all balanced by the "harmless as doves" part, which keeps shrewdness from turning into manipulation.

Now relating it to Business and life

Spot Opportunities Early

Like a serpent sensing movement, a wise businessperson notices trends and market gaps before others do. This means watching closely, listening to customers, and paying attention to the signs.

Protect Your Position

Don't reveal every move or plan to competitors. Serpent wisdom is about keeping your strategy close until it's time to act.

Choose Timing Carefully

Successful deals often come down to waiting for the right moment, whether it's making an offer, expanding, or investing.

Avoid Unnecessary Conflict

The serpent doesn't pick a fight unless it must. Wise business people don't waste energy on battles that don't serve their mission.

Respond, Don't React

Instead of striking back when offended, you pause, think, and choose your words with care, protecting the relationship but not letting yourself be exploited.

Unknown-Author

Read Between the Lines
People often reveal more through tone, actions, and patterns than through words. A wise person notices the undercurrents.

Balance Truth and Grace
"Harmless as doves" means speaking truth without cruelty, even when you see through someone's motives.

Observation Upgrade
Here is a week's plan - see how you go.

Day 1. Goal: Notice more than you speak. - Action: In every conversation today, talk 30% less than usual. Focus on tone, facial expressions, and what's not being said. - Why: Serpents survive by awareness; wisdom begins with sharper perception.

Day 2. Delay the Strike- Goal: Control your reaction speed. - Action: When confronted with a decision or provocation, pause for 5–10 seconds (or longer if possible) before answering. - Why: Quick reactions often serve emotion, not strategy.

Day 3. Protect Your Plans: Goal - Hold Your Cards Close. - Action: Share big ideas or next moves only with those who need to know right now. - Why: Serpent wisdom is partly about avoiding unnecessary exposure to risk.

Day 4. Learn the Landscape: Goal - Understand your environment like a snake knows its terrain. - Action: Spend 30 minutes researching the people, market, or conditions around a current goal before acting. Why: Wise moves require knowing the lay of the land.

Day 5. Blend, Don't Bend: Goal - Adapt without losing integrity. - Action: In a setting where you feel out of place, focus on finding one point of commonality to connect without compromising your values. - Why: Serpents can blend into their surroundings without becoming what they're hiding from.

Day 6. Strategic Silence: Goal - Let Silence Work for You. - Action: In one conversation today, deliberately use pauses to encourage others to fill the gap. - Why: People often reveal more when you simply wait.

Day 7. Gentle Power: Goal - Combine wisdom with kindness. Action: Offer help, encouragement, or valuable information to someone without expecting anything in return, but choose someone trustworthy. - Why: "Harmless as doves" means you win influence through goodwill, not fear. If you follow this cycle regularly, in a month you'll naturally start operating with quiet strength, careful timing, and relational intelligence.

(((((((Dad Joke))))))) No. 3

About 18 months after Dad "won the car," I was due to fly up north again, and I knew it was time for another one. See, Dad had taken on a part-time job as a caregiver. And of course, only my dad would end up with the most demanding client in the whole state, a 24-year-old bloke, built like a brick wall, but mentally about 4. Strong, rough, threatening his carers all the time.

Most people would walk on eggshells. Not Dad. On the first day they met, the young man tried to puff up and threaten him. Dad stood, looked him dead in the eye, and snapped:

"Mate, my last client offered me outside. He's in a f***ing hospital now, busted up. You want the bed next to him?"

The young guy sat straight down, 100% true story. Only my dad would pull a stunt like that. And crazy thing, it worked. They became best mates. Years later, even after Dad retired, the young fella still drops by to visit him. That's Dad. Rough as guts, but all heart.

Anyway... back to the prank.

The kid was eventually transferred to another company because no one else could manage him. But guess what? They poached my dad to follow him. Dad leaves his old job but somehow still collects annual leave from them (typical, always finds a loophole). On top of that, he reckons they'd underpaid him a dollar an hour. He was bragging to me about it, so I thought, beauty... there's my angle.

So, I roped in my cousin's husband, Shane (Shano), for Dad Joke No. 3.

We rang Dad one afternoon while he'd had a couple of beers. Shano Shane) puts on his best "corporate voice" and goes:

"Hello, Mr........ This is John Hanson, general manager of [company name]. I'm calling to offer you a $20,000 termination settlement to finalise your employment, given you've been banking annual leave and your client is no longer with us."

Dad doesn't even hesitate. He goes, "Yeah, sure, mate."

We quickly cut him off: "We legally have to give you time to think it over. Can we call you back in 5 minutes?"

Dad, cool as anything: "Make it 10."

Ten minutes later, we ring again.

"Mr...., our computer shows we underpaid you $1.08 per hour during your time with us. That comes to about $3,790. Of course, this would be on top of the $20,000 settlement."

There's a pause. Then Dad, calm as a cucumber, says:

"... On top of the twenty?"

"Yes, sir."

"Well then... I'll take it."

And that's when I grabbed the phone, dropped the act, and said one line:

"Dad... you're a boofhead."

Silence.

Then, BANG. The worst language I've ever heard in my life came roaring through the speaker. "You bastard! I'm putting you up for adoption!"

He was blowing up deluxe, but three minutes later, he was in stitches, nearly crying with laughter. Said he couldn't believe I'd got him so easily.

And honestly? He's right. What a feeling, even if it was fake, to think you'd just scored $23,000 from a job you'd already left, pure money for nothing.

CHAPTER 25

HEALTH UPDATE

After being home for a week, finding out no prostate cancer, which was great news, but now on blood thinning tablets, what a day today turned out to be. At 6:30 am, I woke up with severe pains in my chest, which within five minutes turned into agony. I thought I was having a heart attack from the blood clots that had been in my lungs the previous week. After spending a week in the hospital, I found myself being rushed in an ambulance back to the emergency department. I thought this was actually the day that I'm going to be knocking on heaven 's door. I genuinely thought this was it, and I'm not that old, so after multiple scans and doses of morphine, it wasn't my heart. It was the blood clots that were in my lung near my heart, causing the excruciating pain and overwork of my heart, so I spent the day in the hospital, living in La La Land, most of the day on morphine.

So, once I got through all the medical checks and they managed my pain, I ended up coming back home and relaxing on some severe painkillers and straight back into writing this book. It doesn't matter who you are. You'll go through seasons and periods, or days, so we have to remind ourselves what is important and what life 's all about. For me, it was nice to spend time talking to my family and close friends, and also to ensure that I'm making the most of my time.

I suppose that's why I believe time is the most important commodity we have, because it is limited and cannot be extended, regardless of the number of days allocated to my life. That's why I don't want to waste one day. What's ironic? I had a late-night phone call from one of my close friends. He's having a tough day because he is trying to get his marriage back together, and I spent an hour just encouraging him, speaking words of life, and giving him some practical wisdom, including the importance of patience.

When you start to help someone else and focus on their problems, it actually puts a smile on your own face and makes you feel better. "When you water someone else, you yourself are being watered! Focus on your own problems - you get down when you try to help someone else with their problems and encourage them to see the light at the end of the tunnel. It will help you realise that concerns and worrying too much don't help a lot. It also helps you forget about your own issues for a time - I call it a stress rest, a mental escape from the world's problems.

Problems Are Part of an Equation

It's true, let me show you.

An equation is just a mathematical sentence with two equal sides, separated by an equal sign. Simple example:

$4 + 6 = 10$

That's all an equation is, a balance of problem, solution, and answer.

Now here's where it gets interesting:

Problem + Solution = Answer

Think about it. You don't need a solution if you don't have a problem. That means every problem carries a solution inside it; it's simply waiting to be worked out.

A New Way to See Problems

At school, I was pretty good at maths, but the further I went, the more complicated equations felt boring and irrelevant. Some formulas felt like they belonged to scientists, not me. But later in life, I realised something: problems are just part of the equation.

That clicked for me. Suddenly, my creative brain woke up. Problems weren't annoyances anymore; they were challenges, half-finished sums waiting for me to complete them.

When I started treating problems like maths, I felt more determined and confident. If there's a problem, then there's an answer, as maths was my best subject. It made even more sense. It may not be immediately obvious, and it may require effort, but the solution exists. That mindset alone gave me more energy and more hope.

How the Brain Solves Problems

Here's the science. Problem-solving and math equations use the same key parts of

the brain:

- Prefrontal cortex (front brain) → thinking, logic, step-by-step solutions.
- Parietal lobes (top brain) → numbers, patterns, spatial reasoning.
- Memory systems (hippocampus) → storing facts and strategies.
- Practice systems (basal ganglia, cerebellum) → making problem-solving quicker and more automatic with repetition.

At first, solving problems feels like heavy lifting. But with practice, your brain rewires itself, making it easier and faster, just like learning multiplication tables.

Confidence Through Practice

When I realised that problems are just equations, I stopped fearing them. I started treating them like practice rounds.

Here's a challenge: ask your friends to send you their minor problems for a month. No pressure, just practice. The more you do it, the more confident you'll become. You'll find yourself thinking, "Okay, this is just an equation. The answer is here somewhere. I just need to work it out."

Big or small, easy or hard, the principle holds. The answer is always there. The only question is: will you be creative enough to find it?

Takeaway Quote:

"Every problem is just half an equation. The answer is already out there; your job is to find it."

Negotiating

This is one topic I really enjoy.

Often, when emotions are high and fresh, it isn't easy to negotiate. Picking the right moment is just as important as the negotiation itself. That's why divorce settlements are so complex, emotions are raw, people feel betrayed, and lawyers make a fortune trying to untangle it.

But good negotiation, to me, comes down to gathering the facts. Get as much information as possible about the deal or the problem. With sufficient information, you can usually find a solution that satisfies both parties.

The Power of Information

Let's say someone is selling a car. They want $10,000. You know it's a great deal and worth more, but you've only got $8,500.

Ask questions:

- Why are they selling?
- How long have they had it?
- What do they need the money for?

The more you know, the better you can negotiate.

If they need $6,000 to fund an overseas move, your $8,500 cash could be just what they need. If they need the full $10,000 for a house deposit, you could offer $8,500 now and $500 per month for three months.

Negotiation always comes down to the "why."

Negotiating Contracts

The same is true in business. Suppose you're negotiating a contract. If the job is urgent and must be done ASAP, then timing is more important than price. You can negotiate a higher rate, but you'll need to work nights and weekends to meet the delivery requirements.

If urgency isn't an issue, you can price it so the job fits neatly into your quieter periods. For you, margins matter. For them, timing may be more critical.

There are always options, but only if you seek out information and engage in honest dialogue. And this is the most significant help in any contract negotiation. Someone you have networked with will assist. Someone you have built a relationship with will make sure you are positioned to get the deal.

Core Principles of Negotiation

Some of the best advice I've learnt blends psychology, communication, and strategy.

- Focus on interests, not positions.

Don't just fight over what someone says they want. Find out why they want it.

- Listen more than you speak.

Silence is powerful. People often reveal more when you don't rush to fill the space. (The old saying: he who speaks last wins.)

- Build rapport early.

People concede more easily to those they like and trust—small talk, shared interests, and ordinary ground matter.

- Always know your Plan B.

Be clear on your bottom line. The more you know your limits and theirs, the stronger you stand.

- Encourage dialogue.

Ask: "What would it take for us to make this work for both of us?" This allows them to feel ownership of the solution and gives you clarity.

- Stay calm, stay professional.

If things get heated, take a break. Don't take it personally. Patience wins more deals than pride ever will.

And yes, sometimes you'll have to negotiate with people who are painful, arrogant, or just plain idiots. Don't stress. Chances are, they already know.

Preparation is Confidence

Knowledge is power in negotiation. Prepare like crazy:
- Know what you want.
- Know what they want.
- Know the market.
- Anticipate objections.

Preparation builds confidence. Confidence communicates credibility.

Win-Win, or Walk Away

The best negotiations end with both sides feeling heard and respected. But remember: sometimes no deal is better than a bad deal.

I've made bad deals before, and I was relieved when they were over. Walking away is sometimes the most brilliant move you can make.

Lesson:

Negotiation is about timing, information, psychology, and patience. Ask why. Listen deeply. Prepare thoroughly. Aim for win-win, but never fear walking away.

Develop Rare & Transferable Skills

In careers, the people who rise are the ones who develop skills that are in demand (tech, healthcare, leadership, finance, communication). Transferable (problem-solving, project management, critical thinking). The more valuable your skill set, the more security and options you'll have.

Now this next part is an essential part of navigating work life - And ultimately it lead me into business and building my own path, partly because of office politics and climbing the corporate ladder - what I've seen people willing to do to other people is just pathetic and a game I just won't play-because I can play it too hard and I won't like myself in this environment but here are some tips as a business owner and also someone who was in the middle of the grind in my 20s-30s.

CHAPTER 26

PLAYING THE INTERNAL GAME

Learning how to navigate workplace politics without losing your integrity is one of the most underrated skills for career growth. Talent and complex work matter, but your ability to build alliances, find mentors, and cultivate champions in your industry will often move your career forward faster than raw skill alone.

Here are some practical rules I teach employees who want to fast-track their careers:

1. Set the Tone with Work Ethic

First to arrive, last to leave. Be at your desk before anyone else, take shorter breaks, and come back before the rest. Always ask your boss before leaving: "Is there anything else you'd like me to take care of before I go?"

Consistency builds reputation. Even if no one says it, people notice who shows up early and who drags their feet.

2. Dress for Respect

Look sharp without trying too hard. My dad used to say, "You demand respect by the way you dress." I don't wear ties, but I make sure I'm the best dressed in the room, whether that's work or going out with mates.

Invest in presentation. A good coat, scarf, and leather gloves are essential in winter. Ladies who present with elegance and effort stand out the same way.

Remember first impressions, every single morning. The greatest compliment a woman can receive? When another woman comments positively on her appearance.

3. Master the Review Game

Performance reviews are tricky; how do you highlight your wins without looking like you're bragging? Here's my strategy:

Pick your top strengths. If there are 10 targets, focus on the five where you shine. For example:

- 1st in recruiting new clients.

- 2nd in time completion of jobs.
- 4th in up-selling/sales.

Present it clearly. One page, bullet-pointed. Title in bold, followed by your ranking. Then outline a researched plan for further improvement.

Lead with humility. Start by thanking your manager for their feedback, then shift to your plan:

"I can see where I'm doing well, but I know I'm capable of more. Here's a strategy I've been working on to push us further, and I'd love your advice on it."

This shows:

- You acknowledge their leadership.
- You want to grow.
- You're already thinking about how to help the company win.

Add Value Beyond Your Job

One of my favourite examples:

Up-selling. "I've exceeded my targets, but if I'm honest, I'm not satisfied with this level. I've researched ways to upsell to our top 20% of clients; statistics show that this approach is three times more effective than selling to new ones. Plus, I've identified areas where we could cut freight costs by 3.5% if we batch deliveries."

Notice what that does?

- Shows initiative.
- Demonstrates you're thinking like a leader.
- Puts you in line for a promotion, without even asking for it.

The Secret Ingredient

At the end of the day, it's about balance:

•Promote yourself without looking like you're self-promoting.

- Brag by presenting data, not opinions.
- Dress sharp, work hard, show loyalty.
- And when the timing is right, speak up, always with humility.

That's how you play the internal game without losing your integrity or your sense of humour.

How to Ask for a Pay Rise

Let's face it, asking for a pay rise is hard. For you, it's nerve-racking. For your boss, it can be uncomfortable too. Why? Because as soon as one person gets a raise, the next three are suddenly at their door asking the same thing (I know it's happened to me as an employer).

But here's the good news: there is a smart way to do it that massively increases your chances of success.

Timing Is Everything

Asking at the wrong time is the fastest way to a "No."

You don't want to bring it up:

- In your performance review (that's the one time they're expecting it).

- When the company is struggling financially.

- On a Monday morning, when your boss is stressed.

You do want to bring it up:

- After the company lands a big client or sale.

- When you know revenue has recently gone up.

- On a Friday afternoon, when people are in a better mood and looking forward to the weekend.

Even the best proposal in the world won't work if your timing stinks. Wait for a moment that is "yes-friendly."

Step 2: Do Your Homework

Before you ask, gather evidence. Research what similar roles are being paid at other companies. Write it down, even print it out and put it in an envelope.

Why? Because it shows:

- You're not basing this on feelings; you've done research.

- You know your value in the market.

- You're serious and professional.

This alone creates a little healthy nervousness in your boss. They know you're not clueless; you're aware of your worth.

Step 3: The Polite Approach (Best for Long-Term Jobs)

If you love your job and plan to stay for years, use this approach:

1. Ask for a short meeting: "Could I have five minutes of your time?"

2. Sit down, thank them for their time, and say something like:

"I really enjoy working here, and I see myself here for the long term. I wanted to show you some research on what my role is paid at similar companies. I'm not asking for the full amount, but I'd appreciate it if you could consider reviewing my salary over the next few weeks. I trust you to be fair."

Why this works:

- You're not demanding.
- You're respectful.
- You're loyal.
- You're giving them space to think.

Bosses don't like being cornered. But they do appreciate loyalty. This method is most effective when you're building your career within the company.

Step 4: The Firm Approach (When You Need Leverage)

Politeness doesn't always work. If your boss is tight with money or always says "not now," you may need to be firmer:

"I've been approached by another company offering me $20,000 more than I earn now. I'd prefer to stay here because I enjoy the team. Is there an amount you'd consider to help me stay?"

What this does:

- It creates urgency.
- It makes them think, "I could lose this person if I don't act."
- It puts the ball in their court without you sounding aggressive.

This isn't a threat, it's just reality. And if they value you, they'll do something about it.

Final Thought

Asking for a raise isn't about greed. It's about knowing your value, timing your request, and communicating it with confidence.

Be respectful, be smart, and be ready to walk away if needed. Sometimes "No" just means not yet.

5: The Gossip Trick (Cheeky, But It Works)

Every workplace has office gossip. You know who it is.

If you let slip to them that you've had another offer, your boss will know by the end of the day. Then, when you ask for a pay rise a week later, the ground is already prepared.

Not the most professional tactic, but hey, sometimes you've got to play the game.

Final Thoughts

A pay rise is never just about money. It's about recognition, respect, and value.

If you prepare correctly, time it right, and approach with either respectful loyalty or firm leverage, you'll give yourself the best possible chance of hearing "Yes."

And remember: if you don't ask, you don't get.

Never Ask for a Pay Rise, Poor People Do This

Okay, I'm being cheeky with that headline, but I'm serious about the principle.

If you're genuinely one of the most valuable people in your company, asking for a pay rise is thinking too small.

Don't Ask for Crumbs, Ask for a Slice

If you're in the top two or three people in your company, the ones who bring in the most revenue, the irreplaceable, don't ask for a pay rise. Why? Because a pay rise is crumbs. A higher salary simply means more tax, while the company still retains the upside.

What you want is equity, a percentage of the company.

That's how CEOs, bankers, and top executives structure their deals. They often take a smaller salary, but they get rewarded with shares or options, and that's where the real wealth is. I read about a CEO who left a corporation recently with $109 million in share options. That didn't come from asking for an extra $10,000 a year.

How to Ask (Without Asking)

So, here's how you play it:

When your yearly review comes up, and the topic of money lands on the table, you simply smile and say:

"I'm not interested in a pay rise."

And then say nothing.

Silence is powerful. It forces them to lean in. "Well then, what do you want?"

That's when you calmly explain that instead of a higher salary, you'd like to discuss a percentage of the company.

Set Targets, Not Tensions

To make it even easier for them to say yes, link your proposal to measurable results:

- "If I increase sales by 10% this year, I receive 2% ownership."
- "If I increase them by 20%, I receive 4%."

Cap it off if necessary, so it doesn't sound greedy, perhaps a maximum of 10% ownership over several years.

This way, they see it not as a gift, but as a win-win deal. They get growth, you get a piece of the pie you helped bake.

Timing Still Matters

Asking for equity is just like asking someone to marry you. Timing is everything.

You don't propose after stumbling home at 5 a.m. from the pub when she's ready to throw you out. You propose after a beautiful wedding, during a season when things are going well, when the mood is right.

Same with equity. Please don't bring it up when the companies under stress or the boss is in a foul mood. Do it when results are strong, energy is high, and you've just delivered a big win.

Why This Matters

Pay rises will only ever lift you a step. Equity will put you inside a lift.

If you're valuable enough, they'll find a way to make it happen. If they say no, that doesn't mean no forever; it might just mean not on those terms, or not yet.

The bottom line? Stop thinking like an employee asking for a handout. Start thinking like an owner asking for your share.

What Is Someone Worth?

People always ask, "What's the maximum salary you could pay someone?" Wrong question.

The real question is: "What's the maximum value this person can bring into my company?"

There is no fixed limit on salary. There is only a limit on the value that can be created.

That's why some people earn $50,000 a year and others $50 million. The number is irrelevant until you ask: "How much money are they bringing in?"

- A salesperson who brings in $2 million a year is worth more than one who brings in $1 million.
- But if you've got a rare talent who can generate $200 million a year in revenue? Well, now we're talking about a mind-boggling salary.

The lesson is simple: never cap salaries and commissions. If you cap them, you're not just limiting the employee, you're capping your company's growth.

Write this on your boardroom wall:

Reward = Results.

The Burger Test

People say, "She isn't worth that much."

I say, "She might be worth double if she brings in the money."

Think about two cooks flipping burgers:

- Cook -A makes 200 burgers a day.
- Cook- B makes 50 burgers a day.

Cook- A generates $2,000 a day for the business. Cook -B makes $500.

Who do you want to employ? Two of Cook A, even if you pay them double. Because results pay for themselves.

That's why "equal pay" sounds nice in theory, but in practice, it can kill growth. Equality means limitations. In the real world, you're paid according to the value you create, not the hours you sit in a chair.

Asking for a Promotion

Now let's talk about promotions. Because just like with pay rises, I don't believe in asking for them.

Why? Because if you're asking, it means you're not ready.

The right way is simple: promote before it's given to you. Make it so obvious that they can't not give it to you.

Here's how:

1. Master Your Current Role

Become the person who consistently delivers excellence. People who can be trusted with small things always get trusted with bigger things.

2. Think Like Your Boss

Don't just tick tasks off a list. Ask: "What's my boss trying to achieve? What problems is the company trying to solve?"

If you can make your boss's life easier, you'll naturally be seen as leadership material.

3. Step Into "Invisible" Leadership

Start guiding without being asked. Lead meetings. Summarise key points. Mentor the new guy. These "invisible" acts show you're already a level above your title.

4. Take Initiative Beyond Your Job Description

Anyone can point out problems; those people should be called CEOs of Problems because that's all they do. The real leaders are the ones who say:

"Here's the problem. Here's my idea for fixing it."

Solutions = respect.

5. Build Relationships, Not Just Skills

Forget the word networking. Build relationships. Trust and friendship move you up faster than talent alone. Promotions stem from being liked and trusted.

6. Show Calm Under Pressure

When things go wrong, most people panic. The promotable ones stay calm, lead, and make things right. That's what bosses want to see.

7. Keep Learning

Take on projects, courses, or challenges that prepare you for the next role, not just the current one. That way, when opportunity knocks, you already look like the best fit.

The Formula

It's simple:

Act like you already have the job you want, before it's offered.

Promotions aren't given to people who ask. They're given to people who are already doing the job in practice.

Final Word

Being an employee doesn't mean you can't build wealth. But understand this: it's easier and far more tax-friendly to build wealth as a business owner.

That said, not everyone wants to run a business, and that's fine. Some people aren't wired for it. But whether you're an employee or an owner, the principle is the same:

- Value creates wealth.
- Reward follows results.

And the best way to get ahead? Don't wait for permission. Don't ask for scraps. Show you're already ready for the next level, and watch the opportunities come your way.

Rising After the Fall: Sacked, Broke, and Starting Again

I don't care how successful you are; life has a way of pulling the rug out from under you. Maybe you've been sacked from a good job, or your business has collapsed. It hurts. It cuts deep. You feel like the air's been sucked out of your lungs, and for a while, you can't even think straight.

I know the feeling. I've lost businesses. I've had people turn their backs on me. I've been in that pit where you wonder, "How the heck do I get out of this?" And let me tell you, those moments are some of the most outstanding teachers of your life, if you're willing to listen.

When you're sacked or when a business fails, the first temptation is shame. You feel like you're not good enough. You think people are whispering about you. You even whisper it to yourself: I failed. But here's the truth: failure is not a person, it's an event. The only way you become a failure is if you stop getting up.

Think about some of the most successful people in the world. Richard Branson has had more business failures than most people have had jobs. Steve Jobs was sacked from his own company. Walt Disney went bankrupt. The list goes on. The difference is that they refused to stay down. Here's what I learned when I went through it:

1. Allow yourself to grieve

Losing a job or a business is like losing a part of your identity. Don't pretend it doesn't hurt. Take a few days to be angry, cry, and punch a pillow if you have to. But then, stop. Don't let it drag out for months or years. Grieve, then move.

2. Strip it back to lessons

Ask yourself: What went wrong? What can I control next time?

For me, sometimes it was poor cash flow management. Sometimes it was trusting the wrong people. Sometimes it was me getting distracted. Brutal honesty with yourself is the best teacher.

3. Reset your perspective

When I lost a business, I thought it was the end. But now I see, it was a reset. It forced me to grow. Sometimes, what feels like a disaster is actually a clean slate. Losing a job might prompt you to start the business you were too scared to start. Losing a business might prompt you to build a smarter, leaner, and stronger one.

4. Start small, start again

You don't have to rebuild overnight. When I was knocked down, I didn't come back swinging with some massive empire. I started small, one step at a time. And guess what? Momentum builds. Small wins bring confidence. Confidence brings bigger wins.

5. Protect your mindset

This is critical. People will doubt you. Some will even laugh at you. That's fine. Let them watch. Protect your mind. Fill it with good books, good voices, good mentors. Switch off the news if it drags you down. Guard your inner circle.

Looking back, getting sacked or losing a business wasn't the end of the world. It was a chapter, not the whole book. Each time, I came back stronger, wiser, more resilient.

If you've been through it or are in the middle of it now, hear me: this is not the end of your story. It's the messy middle. Don't give up. Don't let shame define you. One day, you'll look back and see this season as the very thing that shaped you into who you were meant to become.

You can lose money. You can lose a title. You can lose a business. But as long as you don't lose hope, you can rebuild everything.

The $10k to $200k Blueprint

I get asked all the time questions like-: "If you only had $10,000, what would you do to turn it into $200,000?"

The truth is, most people would blow it. They'd gamble it on the stock market, crypto, or some hot tip from a mate down at the pub. Nine times out of ten, they'd end up with less than what they started.

The wealthy don't think like that. They know $10,000 is seed money. And you don't eat your seed, you plant it.

Step 1: Protect the Seed

When I had little, I learned the importance of not risking everything at once. With $10k, I'd set aside at least $2,000 as a buffer. That way, if something went wrong, I wasn't starting from zero. The remaining $8,000 would become my working capital.

Step 2: Invest in Skills Before Deals

Money follows knowledge. If you don't know how to flip property, trade shares, or run a business, then $10k will disappear fast. I'd spend part of that capital learning a skill that can multiply money. For me, that's been property, small business, and spotting opportunities others overlook.

When I bought into strata maintenance, I didn't just hire staff. I learned how to quote, win tenders, and upsell services. That knowledge grew into a staff of fifty. The skill was more valuable than the money.

Step 3: Play the Small-to-Big Game

You don't need one magic move to go from $10k to $200k. You need a series of wins that compound.

Here's how it works:

- Double $10k to $20k.
- Roll $20k into $40k.
- Roll $40k into $80k.
- Roll $80k into $160k.
- Add some leverage, and you're at $200k.

It's not overnight. But it's achievable. Four or five "doubles" is all it takes.

Step 4: Where I'd Put $10k Today

Property (with Leverage)

$10k can be a deposit on a $100k–$200k property (with finance, not in Sydney or a city). If you add value through improvements such as painting, carpeting, or landscaping, you can revalue and refinance. I've done this before, and it's one of the safest, most proven ways to grow small money into big money. I can hear people already- $10k isnt enough for property. It might be an apartment in the country, another country, etc, or look at doubling it then the property.

Buy, Fix, Flip Small Business

I love this one. For $10k, you can buy a struggling business, such as a cleaning route, vending machines, or even a small online store. Fix the systems, add clients, and flip it for 2–3x more. Repeat it and you're well on your way. Then maybe property!

I did this with strata maintenance. I'd hire staff at $30 an hour, but up-sell their work at $55 per hour. For one person, that's small, but for fifty staff members, that margin adds up to a serious profit.

Digital & AI Plays

This is exploding. With $10k, you can build a digital product, a course, or an AI-powered service. If it takes off, you can scale globally. Yesterday it cost millions to reach people, today you can do it with a phone and Wi-Fi.

High-Risk, High-Reward

Trading stocks, crypto, or options can quickly turn a $10k into a $200k fast. But the risk of losing it all is massive. I only ever risk money I'm prepared to lose in this category.

Step 5: The Power of Discipline

The biggest mistake I see is impatience. People want $200k tomorrow. The smart path is to build steadily, reinvest profits, and keep disciplined.

When I started, I didn't dream of being rich or famous. My dream was to be the CEO of my time, to own my hours. That meant learning to use other people's time, money, and skills. I built multiple businesses, some small and some bigger, and I used each one as a learning experience for the next.

The lesson? With the proper knowledge and discipline, $10,000 can absolutely become $200,000. But it won't be luck. It'll be vision, strategy, and a willingness to do what most won't.

Key Takeaway: Don't chase shortcuts. Double small wins into big ones. Use leverage wisely. And above all, treat money like a seed, plant it, grow it, and reap later. Turning $10K to $200k is hard, maybe impossible in one go-but double 10-20-40… It's possible.

Dealing With a Broken Relationship

A broken relationship can feel like death. The dreams you built together, the future you thought you had, the plans you made, were suddenly shattered. I've been through it, and I know the sting. The empty bed. The silence in the car. The strange feeling of being alone in a place that once felt full of life.

But here's the truth: broken relationships don't have to break you.

Step 1: Feel It, Don't Fake It

Too many people mask their pain with alcohol, rebounds, or burying themselves in work. That only delays the healing. If you've lost someone you loved, whether it's through betrayal, drifting apart, or circumstances, you have to let yourself feel it. Grieve. Cry. Admit it hurts. Healing doesn't start until you're honest with yourself.

Step 2: Learn From It

Every relationship is a mirror. It shows you who you are, the good, the bad, and the blind spots. Instead of just blaming the other person, ask:

- What did I do well?
- What would I do differently next time?
- What standards will I raise moving forward?

This isn't about self-condemnation. It's about growth. Some of my most profound personal changes occurred after heartbreak. Pain can either make you bitter or make you better.

Step 3: Guard Against Desperation

A broken heart whispers lies: "You'll never find someone else. You'll always be alone. You're not lovable." Those are lies. Desperation drives bad choices, rushing into the wrong relationship, compromising your values, or clinging to someone who doesn't respect you.

When I went through breakups, I had to remind myself: I am complete on my own. Another person can add to my life, but they don't define my worth. No one completes you- but some people are great to do life together with.

Step 4: Surround Yourself with the Right People

Isolation is dangerous. Left alone, your mind replays old conversations, old mistakes, old pain. That's why you need solid mates, family, or mentors who remind you of your value. Sometimes, just sitting with someone who cares, having a laugh, or talking things through can help you stay standing when you feel like collapsing.

Step 5: Rebuild Your Life

A breakup isn't just about losing a person; it's often losing routines, habits, even parts of your identity. The fastest way forward is to rebuild your own vision. Start the business, take that trip, get fit, volunteer, try new things. If you only sit around remembering what you lost, you'll stay stuck. Build a future so strong that your past looks small in comparison.

Step 6: Forgive, even if They Don't Deserve It

Forgiveness doesn't mean what they did was okay. It means you're not carrying the poison anymore. I've seen people stay angry at an ex for years, and it consumes them. Let it go, not for them, but for you. Bitterness only chains you to the past. Forgiveness sets you free to love again.

Step 7: Keep Faith in Love

The worst thing you can do is close your heart forever. Yes, it hurts to risk again. Yes, you might get hurt again. But love is worth it. Whether it's with a partner, your kids, your mates, or even strangers, love is what makes life rich. Don't let one broken relationship steal your ability to love fully.

Key Takeaway: A broken relationship doesn't mean a broken future. Feel the pain, learn the lessons, rebuild your vision, and keep your heart open. Often, what feels like the end is actually the beginning of a stronger, wiser, better chapter of your life.

CHAPTER 27

CRYPTO VS PROPERTY VS SHARES

When people ask me about crypto, I always remind them, it's just one tool in the money game. Like property and shares, it has its place. But each plays by different rules.

Property

- Stable & tangible — you can touch it, rent it out, leverage it with the bank.

- Slower growth — but much less likely to vanish overnight.

- Passive income — tenants pay the mortgage while you build wealth.

Shares

- Ownership in companies — you're betting on businesses, not just hype.

- Liquid — you can buy and sell quickly.

- Dividends — some pay you income while you wait for growth.

Crypto

- Borderless — anyone with the internet can own or send it.

- Scarce — especially Bitcoin, with its hard limit.

- High-risk, high-reward — can double in months, or halve in weeks.

The Smart Approach

Wealthy people don't bet the farm on one thing. They spread their money across different asset classes, some safe, some growth, some speculative.

Crypto should never be your whole plan, but it can be a small, exciting part of it. Property builds your foundation. Shares give you ownership in a global business. Crypto? That's the wild card with massive upside if you can stomach the risk.

I personally own all three plus businesses.

I prefer real estate - it's safe, can be improved, and I have control over what it looks like, allowing me to make changes and add income. Has capital growth and income, probably 50% of my worth

I have crypto, and that's ok. But if it crashes overnight, it would be a small percentage of my value.

Shares: I don't claim to know a lot - share trading - it isn't my thing. My research and knowledge about: percentages of losses and no wins versus making Profits I didn't like. I have no influence or control over the value - I hold shares, but I personally know the former director, and he is acquainted with the founder. I was involved as an initial and startup investor. The company's core business focuses on green energy / environmentally friendly solutions, including extensive battery storage (large batteries for cities) and waste purification. Cleans the black smoke from coal-powered plants with a scrubber. I would call this my super-401 (k). This would be 5% of my worth.

My own companies 30%, Strata business, Self-storage units, Mattresses, Lab diamonds, Digital products

13% in other things.

0% modelling Career.

(((((((Dad Joke))))))) No. 4

Two years had passed since Dad thought he had scored that $23,000 "termination payout." He swore black and blue I'd never get him again. But I knew deep down... the old fella was due.

This time, I had to step it up. Go big.

So, I rang a couple of his mates and said, "Look, no matter what, make sure Dad is at the club this Wednesday at 3 pm sharp." They asked why, and I just said, "Trust me. You'll want front-row seats for this one."

The stage was set.

I headed into a costume hire joint in Surry Hills, Sydney. Proper theatre-quality gear. I walked out with a giant curly red wig, a massive red beard, dark sunnies, and an older man's hat.

Think: drunken hairy Irishman vibes. When I looked in the mirror, I didn't recognise myself.

I flew up to Cairns, suited up, shoved a little bottle of water in my pocket, and marched into the beer garden where Dad was sitting with his mates.

I staggered in, grunting and moaning like a drunk. No words, just noises. I leaned onto Dad's table, nearly falling into his lap.

Dad goes, "Sorry mate, someone's sitting there."

I ignored him and collapsed onto the empty chair anyway. He wasn't impressed.

I slung an arm over his shoulder, pulled him close, jostling him a bit. He stiffened straight up, wasn't having it. Perfect.

Then I poured a splash of my beer into his beer, big mistake. If you know old blokes, you know you don't mess with another man's schooner. Dad snapped, "Hey! Don't touch my beer, mate."

I nodded, all innocent. Then stood up, turned sideways, and pulled out my water bottle. I started squirting water onto the ground beside him, shaking my shoulders like I was taking a leak right there next to the table.

His head dropped. He muttered, "Bloody hell… who is this clown?"

When I sat back down, I spotted his little pile of coins on the table, four bucks, maybe. I pinched them.

That was it. He grabbed my hand tight and growled, "Listen, mate, if you don't stop this shit, you're gonna get f***ing hurt."

I stood, shoved my chair into him, and flicked him the bird, middle finger salute right in his face.

That was the boiling point. He leapt to his feet, yelling loud enough for the whole beer garden, "Do that one more time and I'll knock you out!" His legs were shaking, his fists clenched. He was red hot, ready to swing.

That's when I dropped it.

"Jimmy, you're a boofhead."

He froze. Confused. "… Who the hell are you?"

I ripped off the beard and wig.

His jaw dropped. Then he exploded into laughter. Couldn't breathe. Tears running down his face. He said, "Mate, I had no idea it was you. I was about to whack you and honestly, I was bloody scared, because you're a big fella and I'm old now, son!"

The boys at the club were howling. Dad was doubled over, holding his gut.

What can I say? Got the older man's blood pumping again, nothing like winding him up to keep him young.

Confidence: From Embarrassment to Empowerment

The Outsider at the Family Table

I remember sitting at family gatherings and feeling like the odd one out. My mother's (my) family was poor. Government housing. Struggling. To the other relatives, we were almost looked at with pity, like we were the "mistake branch" of the family tree. They loved us, but I'm sure I wasn't on the photo shelf in the early days.

Everyone else seemed better. Better jobs. Better clothes. Better stories. I sat there with nothing impressive to share. I remember Christmas time, when all the cousins would arrive with amazing toys and cool clothes. My older brother and I would always ask our mum to buy our little brother things so he wouldn't feel left out. We were a bit older and understood my mother's situation. I didn't have qualifications. I didn't have achievements. All I had was a past I was embarrassed about.

Confidence Principle: You don't need to be the loudest at the table. Confidence begins when you stop comparing your starting line to someone else's middle.

Leaving Home at Thirteen

When I walked away from home at thirteen, I had nothing but determination to survive. No degree. No plan. Just instinct. I slept rough. I found odd jobs. I hustled because I had to.

It wasn't glamorous. It wasn't inspiring at the time. It was survival. But here's the thing: when you learn how to stand on your own at that age, you build a resilience most people never experience. I love people and my family - I have the best family in the world, and my mother's family is fantastic, beautiful people. Some of my cousins are now like my sisters and brothers, and my aunts are like my second mother. Still, I have learned I can survive on my own and get by. So, although I have many that I love and adore, I

195

don't fear being left stranded or let down. It has become something I can handle and understand that, at times, things happen.

Confidence Principle: Confidence doesn't come from comfort. It comes from surviving what you thought would break you.

CHAPTER 28

JAIL TIME

There was a season when I landed in jail. I sat in that cell facing failure, a lengthy jail sentence, and a stranded family of my own depending on me, but I had nothing but sadness, loneliness, fear, and a loud inner voice asking, "Is this who you really are? Is this how your story ends?"

In that moment, confidence wasn't about pretending I was tough. It was about telling myself, "This isn't the end. I can start again."

Walking out of jail didn't instantly give me confidence, but it gave me perspective: If I could come back from that, I could come back from anything.

Confidence Principle: Confidence is built when you face the lowest moment of your life and still decide it isn't the end.

Divorce

I've sat across the table in a divorce. Papers on the desk. Conversations that cut deeper than any financial loss ever could. There is no winner - one person feels like they sacrificed their soul for the family, working two jobs with no life at all, and sacrificed for what? The other party would feel the same -they gave away a career, the ability to build a financial legacy of their own, and brought up three kids.

When a relationship breaks, confidence takes a hit. You question yourself. Was I good enough? Was I a failure? It is a tough season for both sides. Sometimes it may be tougher on one side.

But there is no winner.

But divorce taught me that confidence isn't tied to whether someone stays or leaves. Confidence is about knowing your worth, even when someone else doesn't see it anymore.

Confidence Principle: Confidence is not about who chooses you. It's about choosing yourself, even when others don't.

Business Failures

I've lost money in business. I've had ventures that looked good on paper and fell apart in reality.

When that happens, the embarrassment is heavy. You worry about public opinion. You imagine people whispering: "See, I knew he couldn't do it."

But failure taught me to stop living for their approval. People talk for a day, then they move on. What mattered was whether I would get up and try again. And I did.

Confidence Principle: Confidence grows when you stop living for applause and start living for progress.

No Qualifications

In a family of fifty people, I was the most unqualified: no trade, no degree, no formal letters after my name. For years, I believed that made me less.

But here's the twist: not having qualifications forced me to find another way. It pushed me to be resourceful, to learn by doing, to hustle harder than the "qualified" ones.

Confidence Principle: Confidence is not in the letters after your name. It's in the courage you carry before your name.

The Embarrassment Shift

For so long, I was embarrassed by my past. I wanted to cover it up, to appear better than I was. But then I realised something: my past was my credibility.

Who do you trust more to teach resilience, someone who studied it in a classroom, or someone who lived it in government housing, jail cells, divorce courts, and failed businesses?

The very things I was ashamed of became the foundation of my influence.

Confidence Principle: Your scars are not a liability. They are your authority.

Practical Confidence Habits

Here's how anyone, regardless of their past, can build confidence: Tell your story honestly. Don't hide. People connect with scars more than perfection.

Take action daily. Do something that stretches you, even in small ways. Stop chasing approval. Most people are too busy worrying about themselves to care about your mistakes.

Re-frame failure. Every loss is training, not the end.

Stack wins. Each small victory becomes a brick in your foundation of confidence. Choose your circle. Spend time with people who see your potential, not just your past.

Confidence Is a Choice

I didn't inherit confidence. I wasn't given it. I built it through trial, error, failure, and rising again.

Suppose you feel unqualified, embarrassed, or worried about public opinion. You're precisely where confidence is born.

Confidence isn't the absence of fear, shame, or doubt. It's the decision to keep moving anyway.

I came from the bottom, and that's why I stand firm now.

Be willing to develop yourself, through experience, reflection, and learning, you might just be the one who steps out of the shadows and leads.

CHAPTER 29

LEADERSHIP

Sometimes it isn't the most obvious one who should be chosen. Often, it's the unknown person in the shadows, the faithful, hardworking individual who is reliable, consistent, resourceful, and committed.

Too often, people chase the yes man, the one who laughs at jokes that aren't funny. We've all seen them come and go. The problem with these types of people is that they have no substance. They can't endure through storms and tough seasons. They have rubber spines.

I observe some of today's leaders in teams and companies, and it's clear that the times have changed. Back in my school days, the big-muscle footballer was the "cool kid." Today, footballers and captains are very different: well-groomed, dressed sharply, intelligent, polite. Many captains are chosen not because they're the most popular or flashy, but because of character and example.

Character First

Character and actions are now the most crucial aspects of leadership, especially in a world where constant cameras and instant access prevail. You can't fake it for long. Society, for all its flaws, has made progress here; it is more open to diversity and more willing to welcome people of different nationalities and races.

But with exposure comes risk. The old saying, "Any publicity is good publicity," no longer holds. In today's cancel culture, even minor mistakes can appear significant when magnified online.

Technology & Leadership

A leader today must also stay aware of the latest technology developments. The pace of innovation, especially with AI, is staggering. You and I may not be able to keep up with every shift, but a wise leader surrounds themselves with people who can. Leadership is not about knowing everything, but about building the right team and harnessing collective knowledge.

And make no mistake: leadership is influence. People want to be part of something, good or bad. I heard a story of a young man who was rejected again and again while trying to join organisations. Out of desperation for belonging, he joined a white supremacist group. He even admitted that if they had rejected him, he would have joined ISIS instead. That's the power of belonging.

This is why leaders must create inclusion. Good leaders make people feel part of something bigger than themselves. It isn't always easy; strong personalities clash, quiet people get overlooked, not everyone gels, but a true leader develops the skill of bringing people in without losing direction.

Leadership in Different Arenas

Different organisations require different types of leaders. Take politics: I almost feel sorry for politicians. Many are unqualified, yet we expect them to manage nations. Part of the problem is structural; we don't pay enough to attract society's best leaders. We have academics and bureaucrats who enjoy the perks but lack the grit to lead through conflict.

Governments grow too big. Bureaucrats waste resources. And politicians bend to popularity instead of conviction. Authentic leadership is often the opposite of popularity. In politics, too often we elect parties rather than individuals, and leaders can be replaced mid-term by their own party. How can a leader govern with conviction when their own seat is always at risk?

In contrast, when I run my companies, I aim to be fair and generous, and I pay staff above award rates. However, I can't please everyone all the time. Leadership requires tough, sometimes unpopular decisions. If I governed like a politician, chasing popularity, my business wouldn't survive.

The Core of Leadership

Leadership requires honesty, courage, and consistency. It's about pushing through storms, standing by your convictions, and guiding others when times are unclear. Families look for leadership. Organisations need it. Teams crave it. Churches depend on it. Leadership matters everywhere.

And the good news? Leadership can be learned.

Today, there are endless online courses, affordable and sometimes even free. I saw one recently: $399 for a year of leadership training with Jordan Peterson and a group of professors, thinkers, and gifted speakers. We live in a time where up-skilling is at your fingertips.

Tip: Keep a record of the courses you complete. Download certificates. Build a portfolio of your growth. It can open doors to positions and roles where formal proof of your leadership journey is valued.

Ten Leadership Topics Worth Mastering

These are the areas the world searches for most when it comes to leadership: timeless, practical, and highly valuable:

Emotional Intelligence & Self-Awareness
- Regulating emotions under pressure.
- Building empathy with teams.
- Spotting blind spots and biases.

Leading Through Change & Crisis
- Adaptive leadership in uncertainty.
- Clear communication when answers are limited.
- Maintaining morale through restructures or downturns.

Building High-Performance Teams
- Turning individuals into aligned, motivated groups.
- Hiring for attitude over skill.
- Creating psychological safety so ideas flow.

Decision-Making & Problem-Solving
- Making smart decisions quickly.
- Avoiding analysis paralysis.
- Balancing data with instinct.

Servant Leadership
- Leading by serving.

- Empowering others instead of chasing credit.
- Growing influence through humility.

Communication & Storytelling
- Inspiring with vision and words.
- Using stories instead of statistics.
- Becoming a deep listener.

Time, Energy & Productivity Mastery
- Habits of effective leaders.
- Protecting big-picture thinking time.
- Delegating with trust, not micromanagement.

Mentorship & Coaching
- Leaders as talent multipliers.
- Growing future leaders.
- Coaching vs. commanding.

Resilience & Mental Toughness
- Handling setbacks without breaking.
- Preventing burnout.
- Balancing grit with compassion.

Vision, Strategy & Innovation
- Turning vision into action.
- Fostering creativity.
- Balancing today with tomorrow.

Hot 2025 Trends
- AI & Leadership — guiding teams in the age of automation.
- Remote & Hybrid Leadership — managing global and virtual teams.
- Inclusive Leadership — embracing diversity and belonging.
- Ethical Leadership — leading with transparency and trust in sceptical times.

Final Word

Leadership is not about titles, muscle, or popularity. It's about character, conviction, and consistency. It's about guiding people toward something bigger than themselves. By developing yourself through experience, reflection, and learning, you may just be the one who steps out of the shadows and takes the lead.

Yes, even when the decisions are tough. The world is crying out for real leaders.

Ways to Make Money

There are three main ways people make money:

1. Sell labour – this is what most of society does, a job, usually 38 hours a week.

2. Sell a product – this industry is growing fast with the rise of online platforms. It's now possible for even teenagers to sell products online. It's actually relatively easy if you know what to sell and how to market and advertise.

3. Sell a service – cleaners, lawyers, trades, and now more than ever, online services. With Artificial Intelligence, even someone like me can play in the IT game.

Before diving into these three, let me say this: industries usually grow slowly, and society has time to train and educate workers to meet the demand. However, I envision a future where an industry will grow so rapidly and advance so far that we won't have enough time to train people for it. AI will have a massive role in this.

Over the last 100 years, we've experienced major shifts, from cars and computers to the internet, digital currencies, and now AI. But I believe what's coming next will be bigger than all past bubbles combined. Technology and innovation are advancing at a pace that outpaces our ability to keep up, but AI can keep up.

Let's examine the three income streams: labour, products, and services.

I reviewed these options and decided to pursue all three, so I wouldn't be dependent on a single industry or sector. I also explored how to structure businesses that could eventually own real estate.

One rule I made early: I will not sell my time. It's my most limited resource. My dream as a young man wasn't to be rich or famous; it was to be the CEO of my time. That isn't easy without money or assets to create a lifestyle that supports it. So instead, I decided to sell other people's time, those who were willing to sell it.

For example, if I pay someone $30 an hour, I expect to receive $55 in return. Otherwise, it's not worth it. That's how I built a strata maintenance business, then three more. As we grew, we had over 50 staff. Even if I only made $10 an hour from each, multiplied by 50, it adds up quickly.

Products: I dabbled in a few. Early on, I tried spearfishing equipment (a passion of mine), but the industry was too small. I worked in glass and glazing for years, but that industry in Sydney wasn't appealing. I built self-storage units, and then I moved into mattresses, which we still sell today. I also got into laboratory-grown diamonds- real diamonds, but grown in labs. I call them IVF diamonds: real, but needing a lab's help to grow. That business is still a start-up, but I enjoy it. Just yesterday, I sold a ring. And now, of course, I'm writing books.

Services: My strata business offered a range of services, including gardening, slashing, cleaning, pressure washing, and carpet cleaning, essentially, anything you could need. Most people (95–97%) make their money through services and labour. However, the best approach, as I discuss in this book, is to build assets rather than liabilities. Once your assets produce more than your expenses, life changes.

One big principle I hold: I don't work in my businesses; I work on them. Once you reach that stage, growth becomes exponential. It's hard to grow when you're on the tools, flat out, chasing loose ends. Many of you reading this are probably nodding right now, because you've felt it.

That's why I decided to include the next chapter; it's for small business owners and the self-employed. Or someone who leads and is responsible for a team of people. These ideas will help you transition from running around like a chicken with its head cut off to delegating, mentoring, and building a team that eventually replaces you.

Next steps

Small Business Owners / Self-Employed

Here are some tools, advice, and lessons that helped me move from "running around like a chook with its head cut off" (working in my business) to delegating, mentoring, and building a team (working on my business).

One of the key areas I see people fail in life is their unwillingness to delegate, train, and equip those around them.

I once read a book by a psychologist that explained the power of delegating. Brilliant concept. Here's how I developed that into my business version.

In a business, there are usually five prominent roles:

1.   Quoting & invoicing
2.   Doing the actual work
3.   Payroll & admin (insurances, super, PAYG, compliance)
4.   Training & managing employees
5.   Sales & lead generation

Think of each one as a jersey, Jersey #1 through Jersey #5.

When you start a business, you usually wear all five jerseys yourself. And let's be real, wearing five jerseys at once is exhausting. It's not unlike trying to play every position on the footy field. You'll get smashed and eventually burn out.

The goal is to hand off each jersey to someone else slowly. That might involve hiring staff, outsourcing, or even partnering with a business.

• **Jersey #1 (Admin/Quoting):** This is usually the first one to take off. You can hire a part-time administrator or outsource tasks such as invoicing, calls, and emails. Even if it's just 2–3 hours a week, it frees you to do higher-value work.

• **Jersey #3 (Payroll/Admin):** Next, outsource payroll, super, and compliance. There are small business accountants and bookkeepers who can handle this at a fraction of the stress it causes you. Once Jerseys 1 and 3 are off your back, you'll feel lighter.

• **Jersey #2 (The Work):** As you grow, you hire staff. At first, you'll still be on the tools, but now you're sharing the workload. Over time, your first employee should be trained not only to work but also to take on some leadership and training responsibilities for others. That's when you start freeing yourself from Jersey #2.

- **Jersey #4 (Training/Managing):** As staff grow in experience, you delegate responsibility and leadership to them. The goal is for your team to run smoothly without requiring you to micromanage.
- **Jersey #5 (Sales):** This is the lifeblood. You might outsource some sales through a lead-generation company, but be careful, many of them are subpar. I have always personally enjoyed staying involved in sales. It keeps me sharp, connected to the market, and aware of what's really happening with customers. However, in the long term, you want systems or people generating sales so that your business isn't relying solely on you.

The strategy is simple: plan how to get each jersey off your back, one at a time. Sometimes you'll share jerseys for a while (half you, half someone else), but the end goal is to wear none of them full-time.

When you finally do, you're no longer "working in" the business. You're working on it. That's when you can oversee all the jerseys, push each area to peak performance, and grow exponentially.

I remember the first time I took off my admin and quoting jersey. Back then, I was flat out, working on the tools during the day, then staying up till midnight typing quotes, sending invoices, and chasing overdue payments. I was tired, annoyed, and felt like I was running three full-time jobs at once.

So, I hired a part-time administrative assistant for just a few hours a week. Honestly, at first, I thought, "This is a waste of money, I could do it myself." But within two weeks, I realised how wrong I was.

Suddenly, I wasn't racing to get home and do paperwork till midnight. She chased the money, sent the emails, and followed up on quotes faster than I ever could. And because she was focused on it, clients noticed the professionalism. Work actually increased.

It freed me to do more of the physical jobs (the tasks that actually generated income). Within a few months, the extra income more than paid for her wages.

That was the light bulb moment: every jersey I could take off would eventually pay for itself, and multiply.

The absolute freedom comes when your business is running smoothly, jobs are being done efficiently, invoices are going out on time, money is coming in, and sales are constantly replenishing the pipeline. Then you can focus on strategy, bigger deals, and maybe even start another business or invest in assets.

That's what makes a business healthy, scalable, and profitable.

I'm sure some of you are thinking this sounds difficult and not easy to achieve - it isn't as hard as you think once you get some momentum - remember that verse I quoted a few chapters earlier.

"A lamp unto my feet" - we don't need to see the end result; we just need to see the next few steps to take. Once we take those 3-4 steps, we can then see the next 3-4. That's life, and as you grow, learn, and acquire knowledge, you will personally come up with ideas and strategies you don't even know about yet. Takes time, commitment, and belief.

It's not that I can't, but how can I?

There is a solution! Are you creative enough to find it or design it? (Yes).

Planning - vision

"Without a clear vision or direction, people lose purpose, discipline, and hope."

Now, I'm not contradicting the lamp theory, but that is relevant for the next steps. This is about having a plan forward with a road map to the destination.

A vision isn't just a dream; it's a direction. Without it, life feels random, like drifting without a compass. I've seen businesses collapse not because the idea was bad, but because the owner had no clear vision of where they wanted it to go. The same happens in families. If a couple lacks a shared vision for their future together, they often drift apart, argue, and eventually break up.

Vision creates focus. Focus creates discipline. And discipline creates results. When you wake up with a vision, suddenly your time, money, and energy line up. You know what to say "yes" to, and what to walk away from.

That's why I believe one of the most significant responsibilities in life is to set a vision for yourself, your family, and your business. Even if it's small at first, it gives you something to grow into.

Now, vision can be something you decide on your own, or you can bring in a quality group of people to brainstorm ideas with you.

Even family members can be a part of shaping the vision; sometimes the best insights come from those closest to us.

For one of my new companies, the vision is simple: grow it, scale it, and then sell it. I don't plan to keep it long-term because I already have assets and don't need to rely on it. That's the catch with selling a business: you either need assets behind you already or a plan to replace that business with another.

A vision is about defining what you want your business to become, its size, volume, expansion potential, and perhaps even a franchise model. All these possibilities can fit into a vision.

Personally, when I plan a vision, I prefer to start with the result and work my way backward. That's just how my brain works. I picture the ideal outcome first, then break it down into steps.

For example, let's take this book. Suppose my vision was:

- Have a hard copy, an eBook, and an audiobook version.
- Build a website to host products and resources.
- Create a mentoring program online.
- Translate the material into multiple languages.
- Package the whole thing -books, digital products, coaching, and seminars, as intellectual property that could even be sold or licensed in the future.

That's a big vision. But once it's clear, I can work backwards into practical steps: below is the usual way people plan. But in reality, I had the whole picture and marketing plan before I even wrote the book.

- Write the book.
- Format it into an eBook.
- Publish the paperback version.
- Record the audiobook.
- Build the website with products and online workshops.

And so on. Each step becomes a building block towards the bigger picture.

Technology also shapes vision. Currently, audiobooks are one of the fastest-growing formats globally. People are busy, on the move, and want to consume content while commuting, at the gym, or doing chores. Just like podcasts, audiobooks are becoming the main way books are "read." That's why timing matters; sometimes, the order of steps needs to shift to meet where the future is heading.

CHAPTER 30

DREAM VS. VISION

A dream is a wish. A vision is a plan. Dreams live in our imagination; they inspire us, but without structure, they fade away. Vision, on the other hand, gives that dream legs. Vision says: This is where I'm going, and here's how I'll get there.

That's why vision is powerful. It's not about "one day" thinking; it's about practical steps that bring the future into the present, piece by piece.

Turning a Dream into a Vision

Asset - let's do this. We should have an example of an asset; it's only fitting.

Say your dream is "I want to buy my first investment property."

- Write It Down Clearly

"I want to own my first property within 2 years that gives me $100 a week positive cashflow."

- Reverse Engineer It

- To buy a property, I'll need a deposit.

- To get a deposit, I'll need to save $20,000.

- To save $20,000, I need to cut $200 a week from expenses or increase income by $200.

- To increase income, I could work one extra shift, start a side hustle, or sell unused items online.

Suddenly, the big, scary dream of "owning property" becomes a simple process: save $200 a week, cut spending, grow your income, research suburbs, and then buy.

- Attach Dates and Accountability

- Savings target: $20,000 in 24 months.

- Property purchased: by the end of Year 2.

- Accountability: Tell a mate or mentor about the plan and check in monthly.

Let's get back to another time in my journey.

My mother and her husband lived in Coffs Harbour, near my grandparents, but they decided to move to Queensland. My mother and her husband then wanted to move back to south-west Sydney. By this time, I was on talking terms with my mum's husband, although we weren't best mates, but we were okay. He never worked due to a back injury, and they had twin boys. They couldn't afford their own place, so my older brother and I decided to rent them a house. We turned the large double garage into a room and lived there.

I was working at a plastic factory called Atlas Plastics, where I was the powder specialist. My job was to ensure that I kept all the machines supplied with bags of small plastic pellets, so they wouldn't run out of plastic to make bottles and large drums. I actually enjoyed working there, and I was only 18, while most of the staff members were around 35 to 45 years old. I got along well with all of them. However, I didn't have a car at the time, and I had to walk about 40 minutes each way. Going to work was okay. But coming home was a pain, all uphill.

So, my brother and I were helping pay the lion's share of the rent, while my mum's partner stayed home, watching TV in the air-conditioned house all day. Well, one steaming hot afternoon, I walked all the way home, walking past his car in the driveway and up the stairs and into the house. I got three steps inside, and my mum's husband started yelling at me to get my stinking shoes off, while in the house, it was really abusive and unnecessary. I was hot, tired, and, come to think of it, also paying the rent.

I barked back at him to shut up and pull his head in. I was no longer a tiny little 13-year-old boy. I was 18, and I was big now. And I had a reputation of being a rough kid in the neighbourhood, and he wasn't getting away with this! And it felt time to pull him up and set things straight; my memory recalled the words he had said to a much younger version of myself. Come outside, and you can have the first punch.

So, I walked over to him, up in his face (with my shoes on). 'Hey, you ……., come outside and you can have the first punch.' The exact words he said to me when I was 13. He put his head down and said nothing. I just laughed and smiled. Now I felt bad for my mother, but this changed everything. He finally knew I was the head of this family, not him. He was never my stepdad; he never tried or wanted to, so he didn't get that privilege.

It's funny that I still laugh at my older brother and my three younger brothers. Because whenever we have family events and parties, my mum's husband will pull up all my brothers and have a go at them if they cross the line with a joke or something, but never me. He knows he doesn't have that place or authority in my life. I became like a dad to my two brothers because we didn't have anyone around to help us grow up. They lost the right to try to reclaim that mantle. He had the opportunity, but he passed it up and moved away, just like my dad did. I can honestly say I love my dad and my mum's husband now, and we get along exceptionally well. However, they both know I brought my brothers up, and they didn't, so they don't have the right or place to interfere.

Let's try to combine all this and explain it!

Thinking

A sharp mind is like a compass. It doesn't just point north once; it adjusts every time the environment shifts. That's what I do: I don't unthinkingly repeat what I've seen before. I reason, weigh options, and if I need to gather more information and knowledge, I go searching. In life, the same principle applies: success belongs to those who know when to pause, learn, and re-aim. - Imagine the sharpest business people suddenly woke up from a 10-year coma and had to get back into business. That's where we are heading if we relax for 1-2 years now. Technology is at the speed of sound. I am about to take us to light speed.

Money

Money is a moving target. What worked last year might not work today. The people who stay ahead aren't just those who know, they're those who keep learning. Just as I can search for new information when needed, wealthy individuals find new opportunities, study emerging markets, and keep their strategies current. Stale thinking is expensive; fresh learning is profitable. I've always been the last to jump on new technology. When emails first came in, I refused for a year; I was not doing it. You can't afford to be like that in business and building assets these days. You have to be moving along. We no longer use horses or sailing boats as our primary means of transportation. They are social outings these days, usually while on holiday.

For example, my company was asked to provide a legal document (just red tape) via email. I pasted the email into ChatGPT, and it generated the document in under 20 seconds. That was $2000 a year ago. If I can, you can!

Real Estate

Property values fluctuate in response to changes in interest rates, government policies, and even the local neighbourhood atmosphere. If you stop learning, you miss the signals. It's not enough to buy land and sit; you must keep watching, researching, and adjusting. The investor who studies constantly will see opportunity where others only see risk.

Here are my thoughts on the near future: governments will adjust and fine-tune all the levers to manage their debts. To ensure the amount of debt being digitally printed is paid and keeps their system running. It has become astronomical like never before. It's the only way to pay back the interest and continue borrowing more. Historically, it is said that all money collapses. Where do I see us heading? Is it digital currency? But how can all countries have their own and compare? They can't. The answer is: #1 worldwide digital currency. The US dollar, as mighty as it has been, won't even come close to the power this digital currency will hold.

You can bank on that!

Money is something that holds value over centuries (e.g., gold, silver, land, productive assets).

• Currencies are government-issued tools to measure and move money, but they almost always decay.

Example Timeline

• Roman denarius: lasted a few centuries, but was debased until worthless.

• Spanish silver real: dominated global trade for 300 years, then collapsed.

• Modern fiat currencies: most launched after WWII; many have already been "restructured," or today we call it the reset, we can't say failed or collapsed.

The near future is clear: governments will continue to pull every lever they can to manage their increasingly impossible debts. They will print, they will borrow, and they will manipulate interest, because it's the only way to survive.

But history teaches us one lesson above all: all currencies collapse. The mountain of digital debt being created today is unlike anything we've ever seen, and it cannot last.

Where does this lead? To a single destination: a worldwide digital currency. Local currencies won't be able to compete or compare, just as ice cubes can't resist the sun. And when it comes, even the US dollar, once the most powerful of all, will look small.

You can bank on that!

Relationships

Relationships need learning, just like money and business do. You don't "win someone's heart" once and then coast along forever. People change. Cultures differ. What matters is the willingness to observe, adapt, and grow.

Looking back, I feel like I've had four versions of myself. At 15, I didn't even like who I was. At 25, I was likable. By 30–35, I was too opinionated, too busy, and focused on being a strong, opinionated leader (but still cute), haha. At 40, I softened. And now, I'm not perfect, but I am calmer, more considerate, less stressed, and much more willing to serve the people I love.

These days, I cook dinner most nights, wash up, or take my partner out dancing by the harbour. When I was younger, I was too busy running a business, raising kids, and chasing success to give much of myself to my family at home.

That's the mistake many couples make: they grow, but they don't grow together. Seasons change, and so do we. But the deliberate effort to change side by side is what keeps love alive.

How I Saved $100,000 with One Change.

Don't skip this chapter.

In business, the two most valuable and limited resources are time and money. If you're starting a new business, or even buying one, you'll quickly realise these two resources can either make you or break you. That's why I've always been obsessed with finding ways to save both time and money.

When I examine a new business, the first thing I do is study the costs. Costs are the silent killers of businesses. Revenue looks good, but if costs aren't controlled, it doesn't matter how much money you bring in; you'll constantly be bleeding out.

Breaking Down Time

Take, for example, one of my companies in strata maintenance and cleaning. At one point, we were managing over 350 sites and locations. Some were new, others were clusters in certain suburbs. The challenge was always: How do we maximise efficiency with time?

We'd look at runs. If a team of four could handle eight large sites a day, or maybe ten, we'd plan their routes so the jobs were close together. Sometimes we'd add a smaller site nearby to make the run more efficient. Every kilometre matters, every extra minute matters.

It's the same with machinery. If a machine is used 20–30 hours a week, I'll buy it brand new, because I know it will be heavily used. But if it's only being used 5–7 hours a week, a cheaper used machine makes more sense.

And vehicles? I've never bought a brand new one in my life. The value drop in the first two years is insane. If a contract is local and requires minimal driving, why buy a $50,000 van when a $6,000 one does the job just as well?

Here's a little trick I've used for years: if I buy vans and Utes under $6,000, I self-insure. Ten vehicles at $1,200 a year would cost me $12,000 annually in insurance. Instead, I take the risk myself. In 12 years, I've only written off one. The result? Roughly $100,000 saved. That's real money, not theory.

The Human Factor

Of course, saving money isn't just about machines and vehicles. It's also about people.

One of the hardest lessons I've learned is that my best worker isn't always my best leader. Leadership is about getting others to perform, not just doing the work yourself. I've had to balance promotions carefully, ensuring

I don't upset someone who feels they are "next in line" while still putting the right person in charge.

And I'm a firm believer that not everyone should be paid the same. Nobody should be underpaid, but some should be overpaid. If two ladies on my team can clean faster and better than everyone else, I'll pay them more. Why wouldn't I? They bring more value.

Smarter Buying

The same thinking applies to equipment. For example, our zero-turn mowers chew through rear tyres. Standard tyres cost $160, but they puncture easily. Then I discovered the new solid rubber/plastic tyres that never go flat. At $500 each, they seemed expensive, until you realise they last the life of the mower. That's savings through smart buying.

Experience has taught me this: don't buy cheap junk. It becomes spare parts in a few months. Buy commercial-grade, buy once. Time has proven it right over and over again.

The AI Game Changer

But the most significant shift I've seen recently isn't in machines, cars, or tyres. It's in artificial intelligence.

My newest toy, ChatGPT, has been nothing short of a game-changer. Let me provide a real-world example.

My son was in Perth recently working on a tender. Typically, tenders are monsters; they take days, sometimes weeks. There are over 40 questions, each requiring detailed answers. Usually, I'd happily pay $5,000 to have one done properly.

But this time, he sent me the questions. I was in the office, waiting around for the police after a break-in, so I decided to give ChatGPT a try. I entered the key information- staff details, current contracts, company capability, and within 30 to 40 minutes, I had a completed, structured response pack. Something that usually takes days was done in under an hour.

That one session probably saved me $2,500 on the spot. And it's not just tenders. We had to write up a constitution, something that usually costs around $2,000 with a lawyer. ChatGPT did it in three minutes.

217

I learned my lesson 30 years ago when I was late to adopt email. I won't make that mistake again. I'm not waiting two years to get on board with AI. The savings in both time and money are too significant to ignore.

The Real Motto

This morning, I couldn't sleep. I've been recovering from blood clots in my chest, so I watched a podcast. Their motto stuck with me:

"Start your business before you're ready."

That resonated with me. It's precisely how I've lived. Don't wait until everything's perfect. Learn, prepare, gather knowledge, and then jump in. You'll never feel fully ready, but you'll be prepared enough.

And the truth is, the businesses that survive and thrive aren't the ones with the most money. They're the ones that master the art of saving time and money while still delivering quality.

Key Takeaway:

If you can save an hour, save it. If you can save a dollar, save it. Over 12 years, small savings can equal $100,000 or more. And now, with AI, the most significant savings are yet to come.

The gold nuggets

1.   "Every dollar you save is a soldier you can send back into the battlefield of business."

2.   "Time and money are your only true currencies; spend both as if your future depends on it, because it does."

3. "AI won't replace entrepreneurs, but entrepreneurs who use AI will replace those who don't."

CHAPTER 31

CRACKING THE CODE!

When people discuss wealth, most focus solely on money. They rarely weigh the importance of tangible assets. Wise investors know how to reduce risk; cracking the code comes from pursuing knowledge and gaining a deeper understanding.

Business isn't just about chasing the next buck. Over time, wisdom will outlast negative opinion.

Nothing worthwhile comes without complex negotiation; relationships will always outweigh the numbers. Every choice stacks like invested equity. Legacy carries far more weight than fleeting luxury. Lean into creating assets and learn to dislike liabilities!

Legacy: What Really Matters

At the end of the day, money, assets, business wins, cars, watches, all of it is temporary. Don't get me wrong, I love a nice car and a good watch. But none of it comes with me when I leave this earth. What does stay is the impact we've had on people's lives.

I've made money, lost money, built businesses, sold businesses, fought with the taxman, fought with myself, and learned a lot of lessons the hard way. But when I look back, the most significant moments haven't been the financial wins; they've been the times I gave something away, or gifted something like the six motorbikes to kids at Christmas. That was joy.

Legacy is not what we leave for people. It's what we leave in people.

Your kids won't remember the brand of car you drove, but they'll remember if you showed up to their game, hugged them when they needed it, and taught them how to think differently. Your employees won't remember every payslip, but they'll remember if you treated them fairly and gave them opportunities. Friends won't remember every dinner, but they'll remember if you listened when they needed an ear.

I've learned that discipline builds, while a lack of discipline destroys. That applies to health, business, money, family, and relationships. A disciplined life creates a legacy that outlasts us.

One day, someone will tell your story. The question is: what story do you want told? That you chased money and ran out of time? Or that you used your time, money, and gifts to make a difference?

I don't want to be known as the guy who made a lot of money. I want my kids and grand-kids to say, "He taught us to think differently. He showed us how to work hard, to be generous, to back ourselves, and to never give up."

At the end of life, none of us are counting dollars. We're counting memories, people, and impact.

So, build wealth. Create businesses. Invest smart. But don't forget the bigger picture. Your legacy is how you made people feel, what you left in their hearts, and whether the world was better because you were here. That's the story worth writing.

As I close off my journey, remember when I was in jail- I said to my father-

"Dad, I don't understand why I'm here or what it's for. But I promise you this: I'll be blessed seven times what I'm worth today. You wait and see." - I was wrong!

I should have added a zero to that number!!!

The "Unknown-Author"

For ongoing support - regular updates and resources coming through the below email-website.

info@unknown-author.cloud

www.Unknown-Author.com.au

Keep an eye out for these upcoming releases:

- Unknown – pastor
- A.I. Will Replace Most Jobs – But Here's What It Can't

For updates and more information, visit: (www.Unknown-Author.com.au)

What if every problem was just half an equation?

The answer is already there — you just need to work it out.

In this book, The Unknown-Author blends laugh-out-loud stories, sharp business lessons, and timeless parables into one unforgettable guide on life, money, and success. From pulling pranks on his dad to negotiating million-dollar contracts, he reveals how humor, creativity, and thinking differently can solve almost any challenge.

Inside you'll discover:

• Why chasing applause is a trap
(and how to build real substance instead)
• The $100K cost-cutting secret that every business owner should know
• How to use A.I like ChatGPT to save days of work in under an hour
• Why liabilities lie, assets work, and how to make money multiply
• Parables like The Hidden Painter and Big Bucks, Small Bucks that will change the way you see success

The question isn't if solutions exist. They do. The real question is: will you be creative enough to find them?

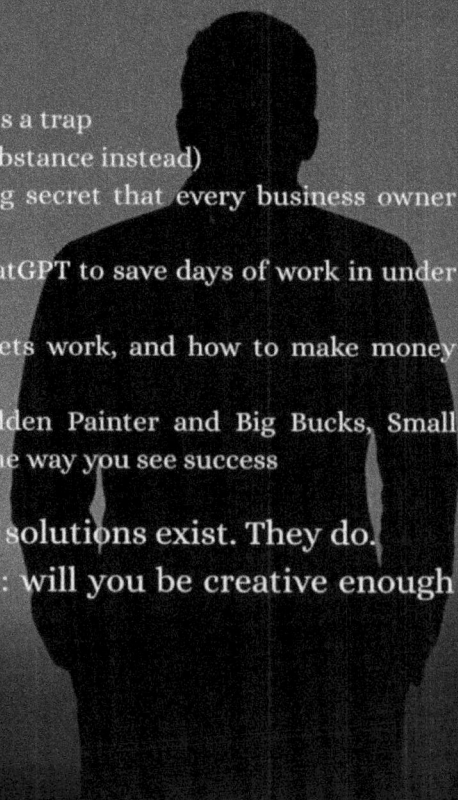

www.ingramcontent.com/pod-product-compliance
Lightning Source LLC
Chambersburg PA
CBHW071727200326
41519CB00021BC/6607